The Answers of Jesus to Job

D1526895

THE ANSWERS OF JESUS TO JOB

BY

G. CAMPBELL MORGAN, D.D.

BAKER BOOK HOUSE
Grand Rapids, Michigan

Reprinted 1973 from the edition
published in 1935 by
Fleming H. Revell Company

Fifth printing, July 1981

ISBN: 0-8010-5917-8

Printed in the United States of America

CONTENTS

THE ANSWERS OF JESUS TO JOB

I

INTRODUCTORY

" There was a man in the land of Uz, whose name was
Job ; and that man was perfect and upright, and one that
feared God, and eschewed evil."—Job i. 1.

In magnificence of argument and beauty of
style, the Book of Job is one of the greatest in
literature. It is surrounded by clouds of
mystery as to authorship, as to the characters
presented, and as to the period of its writing.
Moreover, there have been almost endless dis-
cussions as to the ultimate purpose and value
of it. In earlier days of dealing with the book,
I described it as " The problem of pain." I
think that may abide, but if it presents the
problem of pain, it does not afford any solution
of the problem. It is very difficult, and perhaps

impossible, to crystallize into anything like a brief statement the purpose of the book.

Nevertheless its value is that it is the Book of Job. That is to say, it is the story of a man. Everything gathers around that central fact; and as we read, we see this man related to the spirit world, accessible to the approach of spiritual forces outside his own personality both for good and evil. In other words, God and Satan are revealed as interested in this man. We see him also related to other human beings, his wife, and a little group of friends gathered round him. Many acquaintances are referred to, but they disappear, very quickly disappear, as acquaintances do in circumstances such as those in which Job found himself. But supremely we see him within the consciousness of his own personality. One great element of the book is that all things seem to retire, or to be retired from him, until he is alone with himself.

It is to this last phase of the revelation that I propose to devote a series of studies, Job within his own personality. Whereas as we move through, we shall hear the voices of the philosophers talking to him, we shall pay little attention to them. Eliphaz and Bildad and Zophar, and that fine young man who appears at the end, Elihu, will all be heard ; but we shall do with them very largely what we have often to do with the philosophers, let them talk, while we attend to profounder matters !

I submit then, by way of introduction to these meditations, that as we take our way through this book, ever and anon we hear this man Job say things which arise out of his own deepest elemental experience. He replied to the philosophers. Thank God he did. But ever and anon, in the midst of his speech to those who were arguing with him, there welled up from the deepest of his consciousness, some challenge, some cry, some inquiry. Those are the things to which we want to give our special attention. Each one of them is elemental, and affords a deep insight into human nature.

The general thesis of our meditations is that of the answers of Jesus to Job. If there be no New Testament, or if we take away from it its essential value in its presentation of Christ, then we still have the Book of Job ; it will remain in literature, but it will be the record of an unanswered agony. There is no answer to Job till we find it in Jesus. But we find an answer to every such cry of Job in Jesus.

As an introduction to this line of consideration, it is important that we refer to what we see of the man, as to his surroundings, his relation to the spirit-world, and his relation to human beings, in order that presently we may listen to him.

First, then, let us see the man. We are told his name. We are told that he came from, or belonged to, Uz. About Uz we know practically nothing. Such a place is mentioned in Genesis. Whether it is the same or not does not matter. The name passes and the location passes. It is the man we want to see. He is at once revealed in the words, " That man was perfect and upright, . . . one that feared God and eschewed evil." Two words thus describe the man ; and two phrases tell us the secret of his being what he was. The man is described as " perfect and upright."

We must not read into that word " perfect " all that our English word may mean. It does not mean at all that he was a sinless being.

The word "perfect," the Hebrew word, simply means complete ; he was complete. I think I will put the thought of that word into a phrase with which we are quite familiar. I do not know that I like it, but it will help us. It means he was an all-round man in the best sense of that word.

But more, he was "upright." The Hebrew word means straight. He was an all-round man, and he was straight. I do not know that we could pay any man to-day a higher compliment than to say that of him. The statement so far has not touched upon his relationship with God. It has had to do rather with his human relationships. Job had nothing in him that his fellow-men could bring as a charge against him. He was complete and straight.

But the recorder also gives the secret of this uprightness or completeness of Job. He says he was one "that feared God." That is religion. "And eschewed evil." That is morality. The two things are put into juxtaposition of statement, as they always are in fact. That is the ultimate meaning of the word of Jesus ; the first law, " Thou shalt love

the Lord thy God "; and the second like to
it, " Thou shalt love thy neighbour as thyself.
On these two commandments hangeth the
whole law and the prophets." Morality is ever
rooted in religion. A man who is an all-round
man in the true sense of the word, and who is
known to his neighbours as a straight man, a
man against whom men can bring no specific
charge, that man has dealings with God. He
" feared God." And he turned down evil—
yes, that is it exactly—eschewed. He turned
down evil. A man with an upward outlook,
and from the upward look he learned how to
deal with all the things by which he was surrounded ; he turned down evil.

The remarkable fact is that according to the
record, that estimate of Job was ratified by
God Himself. God said to Satan the same
thing about him : " A perfect and an upright
man, one that feareth God, and escheweth
evil." That Divine estimate is intensified,
because God said of him, " There is none like
him in the earth."

So we are brought face to face with a man
of integrity, a man of uprightness, a man
having relationship with God, turning down

evil wherever it presented itself. It is very important we should remember that.

Now for the story. We watch this man, and we do so in the realm of the physical, in the realm of the mental, and in the realm of the spiritual. This man, straight and complete, fearing God, turning down evil, is seen visited by Satan, and, as a result, swiftly came overwhelming calamities. The reason of these calamities is not to be found in the man himself. That is the mistake courtly Eliphaz, and argumentative Bildad, and blunt Zophar made. They all believed that the reason of his calamity was something in himself. The book introduces him in such a way as to make it perfectly plain that it was not so. We see Job stripped of everything upon which man naturally depends on the side of the natural. Stripped of wealth, suddenly reduced from opulence to penury. Stripped of his children, who are swept out. Stripped of his own health. The vim and the virility and the vigour of his manhood all taken from him, sapped away. Presently the stripping goes further, and he loses the partnership of love in faith. I am referring to the story of his wife. Don't let us criticize her until we have been where she was. See what it meant to him. So far, wealth gone, children gone, she had stood by ; and then there came the moment when her love-lit eyes looking at her man in agony, physical agony, she said, "Renounce God, and die." Which meant, I would rather know you were dead, than see you suffer. I sympathize with her. So does every woman. Yes, but get into Job's soul. She who had stood by, the companion of his faith, for very love of him is suggesting to him that he abandon his faith. He is stripped of her partnership in faith.

And still the process runs on, and it is a long one. His friends—he loses them. They came. It is an old, old story. One has often said it, but I am going to repeat it. I like these men ; I like Eliphaz and Bildad and Zophar for two or three reasons. I like them first because they came to see him when he was in the darkness, when the other crowd of acquaintances had all gone. Then I like them because when they came into his presence they sat still and shut their mouths for seven days. That is a great proof of friendship, the ability to say nothing. And yet again, when they did speak, I like them because they said everything they had to say to him, and not to other people about him. The only mistake they made was that they tried to put him into a philosophy that did not hold him. He welcomed them, he was so glad to see them that he poured out his soul in a great wail of agony which he had been nursing, and then he found that they did not understand him. He lost his friends.

That brings us to the mentality of Job, his own personal consciousness. There was rooted in him a conviction of integrity which was assailed by his friends. He was misunderstood. Perhaps there is nothing worse in human life than that our lovers should misunderstand, when we cannot explain things, try as we will. In the case of Job the result was that presently he lost the sense of the greatness of his own personality. At the beginning, in the midst of the agony, he had said, " Naked came I out of my mother's womb, and naked shall I return thither." As though he had said, I am still there, whatever happens. But he lost this, and cursed the day he was born. And yet more In the gloom and darkness, he lost his sense of God as just. He never lost the sense of God in some ways ; but he did lose his conviction that God was just. God, yes, always God ; but surrounded with fog and mist and mystery. God became the tragedy in his thinking. Thus we see the man : physically stripped ; mentally misunderstood ; and therefore spiritually, all the way through struggling, groping after a solution of God as the One Who was dealing with him.

Thus, taken as a whole, with that tragic background, this Book of Job faces a fact which is everywhere apparent in human life, and which still causes perplexity. What is it ? That there is suffering, and sometimes tragic and terrible suffering in the world, which is not the result of the sin of the sufferer. In this great central book of the Biblical literature, in this drama of Job, that great fact is faced : a man suffering, not because he has done wrong. We are still facing it everywhere. In every land, in city or in the country, we are faced by people thus suffering. I see at this moment in a cottage in the country a girl lying on a bed, where she has lain for twenty-eight years, suffering through no sin of

her own. Thank God many flowers are there.
But there she lies suffering through twenty-
eight years. That is the background of this
book.

If the final light may not be clear, I suggest
that it shows that a human life has wider
values than that of its own existence or experience ; or rather, that out of the experiences of
one life, there may be wider, higher values
than the individual at the time may know. I
will content myself now with saying one
thing only. Through this man's suffering
the devil's blasphemy against humanity was
denied.

In the dramatic scene at the beginning,
transactions in the spiritual world are revealed.
The sons of God present themselves before
God, the term " sons of God " being equivalent
to angelic beings, the messengers of God.
Among them came Satan, angelic, but fallen :
and God asks him, " Whence comest thou ? "
There is tragedy in his answer. " From going
to and fro in the earth, and from walking up
and down in it." That reveals the endless
restlessness of evil. Then came the question
of God. " Hast thou considered My servant

Job ? "   " Considered " is a very strong word.
It means, Hast thou been watching him ?
Hast thou been examining him ?   Hast thou
been going round and round the citadel of this
man's soul, trying to find some way to break
in ?   " Hast thou considered ? "   Now listen
to Satan.   " Doth Job fear God for nought ? "
That is the devil's blasphemy against human
nature.   He runs on.   " Hast Thou not made
a hedge about him, and about all that he hath
on every side ? "   That was true.   Said the
devil, " Thou hast blessed the work of his
hands."   Perfectly true.   " And his substance
is increased in the land."   And that also was
true.

But listen again :   " But put forth Thine
hand now, and touch all that he hath, and he
will renounce Thee to Thy face."   The devil's
blasphemy against humanity was that man
serves God for what he can get out of Him.   It
is an old song, but it is set to many a modern
tune.   They are still saying it.   Much of this
scintillating brilliant nonsense that is being
published in the form of fiction, and in essays
to-day, is saying the same thing.   They say
a preacher is continuing to preach what he does

not believe, because he is afraid of losing his living! They say the old lady goes to church, because of the blankets given away at Christmas. The same thing is meant when clever people talk about the rice Christians in China.

God said in effect, ' Go to! try it out ; take away everything.' Thus Job is a battle-ground between God and Satan, between heaven and hell, between the truth about human nature at its deepest and the lie the devil is telling. Job went through all the process with an honesty that is the more magnificent, because at times he was hot in protest, and cried out to God for justice, and asked Him to maintain his integrity. In the end, the hissing lie of Satan the serpent was answered.

In all this there is permanent value. There are many who do not know the ultimate meaning of the experiences through which they are passing to-day. They are hidden away, with some suffering, some agony, some trouble gripping their hearts ; not the result of their own sin. They say, What is God doing? I cannot tell them. But this book suggests that there is a meaning, and there is a value.

Job through all his agony stood up, and the
literature telling the story has come down all
the ages, giving the lie to the devil's lie about
humanity. I think it is fair speculation, that
Job, in the life beyond, will be thanking God
for all he passed through, if he made that
contribution to the truth of God about the lie
of the devil.

Taking the book as a whole, it certainly has
this value also. It proves the inadequacy of
human thinking in the presence of human
experience. This is true both in the case of
the philosophers, and in the case of Job himself.
We listen to the philosophers, Eliphaz, and
Bildad, and Zophar, and that wonderful young
man Elihu, who began by saying, old men are
not always wise ; and then did some marvellous
thinking. If we study all the speeches of
Eliphaz and Bildad and Zophar and Elihu, we
shall not find anything to object to in what
they said. Their philosophy was perfectly
correct and true so far as it went. Who will
quarrel with Eliphaz when he says, " Acquaint
now thyself with Him and be at peace ? "   All
they said was true. But there stood a human
soul, stripped and in agony, and all they said

never reached him, never accounted for him. His experience defied the thinking of the philosophers.

It defied his own thinking, too. He thought as furiously as his friends, but he got no solution until there came a day in the magnificent drama when God first broke across the speech of the philosophers, and silenced them.

Just as Elihu was in the midst of his eloquence, God said :

" Who is this that darkeneth counsel
By words without knowledge ? "

I think that is what God is saying to-day as He is listening to some of the philosophers. Who are these that darken counsel by a multiplicity of words ? They may be honest, sincere ; but human experience sometimes is too big for definitions, and laughs at philosophers, in its agony.

All this is equally true of Job. He tried and could not understand, and all his speeches reveal his ignorance of the deepest meaning of his own experiences.

One other thing. Taking the book as a whole,

it presents a universe in which, whatever the problems, God is seen as supreme. There is no greater book in the Bible on the ultimate sovereignty of God than this. It may not explain all His methods, but it reveals Him as present and acting. Satan, the arch-enemy of all, wanting to prove that God blundered when He made man, suggesting that a man only fears God because of sycophancy, because of what he can get out of Him. The devil with a lie, and eager to prove his own lie. But mark the dramatic majesty of it. He cannot touch a hair upon the back of a single camel that belongs to Job, until he has Divine permission. God is throned high over evil. It is a universe in which God reigns. There is a moral centre to, and basis of, all things. That is the vision that made Browning sing what some of us so often quote, because we love it so :

> " That what began best, can't end worst,
>   Nor what God blessed once, prove accurst."

In a final word, concentring attention upon Job, what does the book show ? A man stripped to the nakedness of his own personality, stripped to the nakedness of his own being, divested of all the things which clothe the spirit ; divested of all the things upon which a man depends as he takes his way through life ; those precious things—possessions, and children, and health, and love in comradeship with faith, and the friends that gather about us, and the conviction of the greatness of our own personality, and of the justice of God—Job lost them all. We see a man in the appalling majestic loneliness of his own being. Watching him, we listen to him.

In doing so I am more than interested, I am arrested and held, by the splendid argument of the man as against the insufficiency of the philosophy of his friends. But I hear more. Every now and then great essential and elemental cries come up out of the centre of that personality so stripped and lonely ; cries of need, cries of inquiry, cries of challenge. Then I shut the book and find no answer to one of them. It is a great thing to have heard them. It is a great thing to have had that unveiling of human need, but there is no answer.

Then I turn to the New Testament, and I see one Jesus, Who began without any wealth,

Who went through life largely devoid of the things that others depend upon. But before I am through with Him I find He has answered every question Job asked, and supplied every need that Job revealed. So. we will consider the answers of Jesus to Job.

II

THE CRY FOR A DAYSMAN

" There is no daysman betwixt us,
That might lay his hand upon us both."

Job ix. 33.

" There is one Mediator between God and man, the Man
Christ Jesus."—1 Timothy ii. 5.

WHATEVER the dramatic interest in the Book
of Job may be, and it is great ; whatever
interest we may find in listening to the eloquent
addresses of the philosophers, or the impassioned
responses of Job, the final value of the book
lies deeper. That is to be found in the fact
that here we see a man stripped to the nakedness
of his own individuality ; and as we listen to
these men talking to him, and to his replies
to them, ever and anon through the process
some great cry comes up out of his essential
elemental human nature.

The first of these cries which arrests me is
found in these words :

" There is no daysman betwixt us,
That might lay his hand upon us both."

This occurs in the first cycle of controversy between Job and his friends, and in the course of his reply to Bildad. Bildad had argued, and quite correctly argued, that God must be just. Job commenced his answer by agreeing so far, as he said :

" Of a truth I know that it is so,"

and followed this declaration by asking a question :

" How can a man be just with God ? "

It is of vital importance that we should understand that question. It does not inquire how a man can be justified before God. It was a forensic question, a word of the law-court. Job meant, How can a man argue his case with God so as to justify himself ? His friends had declared that he was suffering on account of sin. His inquiry was as to how he could argue his case with God, so as to prove that this accusation was false. Continuing, he gave his reasons why it was impossible ; and it was then that this great cry came out of his life :

" There is no daysman betwixt us,
    That might lay his hand upon us both."

The cry revealed Job's apprehension of the only way by which a man could have dealings with God. Our method of consideration will be that of considering the cry, and then showing how the final answer to the need revealed is found in Jesus, covering the ground by the consideration of the two texts brought thus into juxtaposition.

> " There is no daysman betwixt us,
>   That might lay his hand upon us both."
>   " There is one Mediator between God and man, the Man Christ Jesus."

The cry of Job was born of a double consciousness which at the moment was mastering him ; first, that of the appalling greatness and majesty of God ; and secondly, that of his own comparative littleness. This was not the question of a man who had dismissed God from his life and from the universe, and was living merely upon the earth level. It was rather the cry of a man who knew God, and was overwhelmed by the sense of His greatness. As he ran on, he illustrated this in such sentences as, He "removeth the mountains," "He overturneth them in His anger," He "shaketh the earth out of her place ; and the pillars thereof tremble. He commands the sun," and so forth.

Over against that was the sense of his own comparative smallness. He felt he could not get to this God. He was altogether too small.

The Hebrew singer, David, had the same feeling from a slightly different angle when he said :

> " When I consider Thy heavens, the work
>   of Thy fingers,
>   The moon and the stars which Thou hast
>   ordained ;
>   What is man that Thou art mindful of him?
>   And the son of man, that Thou visitest
>   him ? "

There we have the same double consciousness, that of the greatness of God, and the comparative littleness of man. There was a difference, however, in that David asked how can so great a Being notice so small a being; while Job's was rather, How can so small a being have dealings with so great a Being ?

Out of that double consciousness came this sense of need. The fundamental necessity was to get to God, but that to Job was the difficulty ; and here there flashed forth this cry revealing the sense of the need for a daysman. To bring the idea into more modern terminology, it is as though Job had said : There is no umpire, there is no arbiter, there is no one who can stand between us, interpreting each to the other; me to God, and God to me. There is no one to lay his hand upon us.

The laying of the hand suggests the imposing of authority on both, on the basis of a true interpretation of each to the other.

Here, then, was Job crying out for some one who could stand authoritatively between God and himself, and so create a way of meeting, a possibility of contact.

It is indeed a great cry found in this ancient writing. Many centuries have gone since the book was written and that cry escaped the human heart. Nevertheless, it is a cry of elemental human nature, and expresses an abiding need.

Man's nature demands God for the full realization of itself. No man can live in the full sense of the word, unless he has conscious dealings with God. It is true that God has dealings with every man. There is no escape from Him. No single life on the earth is removed from God. He is the God in Whom we live and move, and have our being ; and that quite without regard to our attitude towards Him. To use an old and familiar illustration. In the dark and disastrous night when Belshazzar and his lords were given to drunkenness and obscenity, Daniel, before giving him an interpretation of the handwriting on the wall, said, " The God in Whose hand thy breath is, and Whose are all thy ways, hast thou not glorified."

This fact of contact with God is not enough for the realization of life. The fact that God makes His sun to shine so as to heal and to bless, without reference to character, does not in itself ensure the full realization of life. Life only becomes complete when man has dealings with God directly, and consciously. That is the true dignity of life. All the tragedy of human failure results from the fact that man has come to think of himself meanly, instead of magnificently.

This being granted, we also have to face a universal sense of distance ; or of some discrepancy between God and man, so that men are not able to have conscious communion with Him. Prayer seems to be an utterance to the void, with no answering voice. Therefore, when by reason of strain or stress of any kind, man becomes conscious of his need for communion with God, at the same moment he is conscious of his need for some intermediary. This was the deepest meaning of the cry of Job :

" There is no daysman betwixt us,
That might lay his hand upon us both."

We now turn from the elemental cry of Job, and from the Old Testament, to consider the apostolic word concerning Jesus. " There is one Mediator between God and man." That is the Gospel in brief. That is Christianity fundamentally. Said Job, " There is no daysman." The answer is, " There is one Mediator." Elemental humanity, aroused to a sense of the necessity for God, a consciousness that God cannot be reached, cried out for some one to stand between them. At last in clearest tones the answer is found in the declaration that such a One is found, " the Man Christ Jesus."

Let us examine this a little closely. The word "Mediator" conveys exactly the same idea as the word "Daysman." I do not quite like the word that first suggests itself to me, but reverently I will use it ; it means a middle-man ; or as we have already said, an arbiter ; some one standing between man and God, some one who puts his hand on man and on God ; some one who lays his hand on God with authority, the authority of partnership and fellowship ; the authority of the fact that He is one with God, and enters into all the Divine counsels, and One Who lays His hand on me with the same authority, authority based upon the fact of His own humanity, that He knows human nature, not merely with the intellectual knowledge of Deity, but with the experimental knowledge of the Incarnation. "The Man Christ Jesus" thus lays His hand on God and on man.

But again, of this one Mediator we are told that He "gave Himself a ransom." At once we reach the point of light and interpretation. It is not merely that He is Divine and human, but that by Him something has been done which makes the way of approach to God possible.

The implicate of the declaration becomes a revelation. What is it that separates between man and God ? A Hebrew prophet once addressing the people of his own nationality, uttered these significant words, " Behold, the Lord's hand is not shortened, that it cannot save ; neither His ear heavy, that it cannot hear." That is to say, if it be that man is unable to reach God, God can reach man, and hear him. Then the prophet gave the reason for this inability on the part of man. " But your iniquities have separated between you and your God, and your sins have hid His face from you, that He will not hear." That is the reason of man's failure to get to God, and to have dealings with Him. The ideal man, that is, man according to the Divine purpose, needs no arbiter between himself and God. A sinless man needs no mediator. He will not cry out for a daysman. Ideal man walked with God, and talked with God. That was true of man as he was created according to the Biblical revelation.

When we overleap the centuries or the

millenniums, as the case may be, we find God's Second Man. He needed no arbiter between Himself and God. He walked with God and talked with God everywhere ; heard the beauty of the Divine message in the songs of the birds, and saw the Divine glory flaming in flowers.

The reason why man is conscious of his inability to thus commune with God is that something has intervened. There has been a rupture, and there is therefore a lack of articulation. Man was created to walk and talk with God, to think the thoughts of God after Him. All human success along the lines of science simply comes from the fact that man is struggling after that very thing. Nevertheless all the while there is a definite hiatus, a gap, between man and God. Again, according to the Biblical account, that rupture was created when man fell from the spiritual to the psychic. He lost touch with God by reason of his rebellion against the government of God. By that rebellion he lost his sense of God, and the sense of his own spiritual nature. This is not to say that the psychic or the mental is essentially wrong ; but it always fails when it is divorced from the spiritual. When man descended by rebellion to the level of the merely mental, he began a quest after God with the powers of his mind, and has never been able to find Him.

Turning over the page in this Book of Job we hear Zophar speaking, and he said to Job :

" Canst thou by searching find out God ?
Canst thou find out the Almighty unto perfection ?
It is high as heaven ; what canst thou do ?
Deeper than Sheol ; what canst thou know ? "

The struggle of humanity to make contact with God through searching with nothing other than the mental occupied in the search, is always a failure, and is disastrous.

It is at that point that Jesus comes in with His answer. "There is one Mediator between God and man, the Man Christ Jesus, Who gave Himself a ransom." The word *antilutron*, here rendered "ransom," occurs only at this point in the whole of the New Testament. Moreover it is a word unknown in classical Greek. It ever seems to me at this point Paul almost coined a new word. Nevertheless, I find something very much like it in Matthew and in Mark. That is to say, they both report Jesus as using the word *lutron*, as He said that the Son of Man had come to " give His life a ransom for many."

An examination of the word shows that it refers to an activity wherein and whereby the sin which has shut us out from God is taken away ; and so an activity wherein and whereby we are brought back, out of the realm of the merely mental into that of the spiritual. Thus the way to God is open. Therefore He is the Daysman.

By that intermediation He restores the possibility of direct and immediate fellowship with God. When man yields himself, not theoretically, but actually, to the Man Christ Jesus, Who is the Mediator, he finds that the evil that had blinded him, and made him insensible of God, is removed ; and direct dealing with God becomes not merely possible, but an actual experience. As Paul says in another of his letters, "we have access " through Him to the Father. Such access means not merely knowing much about God, but knowing God.

It was indeed a great cry which Job uttered, born of his sense of lack of first-hand contact with God ; and the cry has found its full and complete answer in the One of our humanity, and yet Himself one with God, Who becomes a Mediator, laying His hand with ultimate authority upon God, and upon man, thus bringing them into conscious fellowship.

III

THE INQUIRY AS TO LIFE

" If a man die, shall he live ? "—JOB xiv. 14.

" He that believeth on Me, though he die, yet shall he live."—JOHN xi. 25.

THESE words of Job occur in the first cycle of his controversy with his friends, and are part of his answer to Zophar. Zophar had bluntly re-affirmed the view expressed by Eliphaz and Bildad, that Job's suffering must have issued from his own sin. The answer of Job was a lengthy one, occupying in our arrangement, chapters twelve, thirteen, and fourteen. His mood is clearly revealed in the way in which he began his answer, with a note of satire in the midst of his pain and misery and loneliness and darkness. He said :

" No doubt but ye are the people,
And wisdom will die with you."

He then declared his determination to appeal from them to God. Completely dismissing

them, all the rest of his answer is of the nature
of such an appeal ; and right in the midst of
it these words occur. They are essentially
parenthetical. That is to say we might leave
them out, and yet not interfere with the main
line of his argument. It was a great outburst,
evidently out of some deep consciousness,
creating a wistful wonder. It came out of the
essential fact of his spiritual nature :

" If a man die, shall he live ? "

Continuing, he said in effect that if he were
sure that were so, he could bear up under
all the trial. That is what he meant when
he said :

" All the days of my warfare, would I wait,
Till my release should come."

Evidently, although he asked the question,
he had no confidence that the answer would be
in the affirmative. This is revealed in the fact
that he at once relapsed into language dolorous
and full of despair :

" But now Thou numberest my steps ;
Dost Thou not watch over my sin ?
My transgression is sealed up in a bag,
And Thou fasteneth up mine iniquity.

> And surely the mountain falling cometh
>   to nought,
> And the rock is removed out of its place ;
> The waters wear the stones ;
> The overflowings thereof wash away the
>   dust of the earth."

and so forth. Out of the midst then of that dark and mysterious outlook, came the cry :

> " If a man die, shall he live ? "

It was only a suggestion, which for a passing moment at least cast a gleam of light through the gloom in which he was living. As we have said, the gleam was almost immediately overwhelmed with the gloom, but it had shined forth. It was a question of agonized humanity out of the midst of mystery. It was only a question, but what a question !

There was no answer to that question until we hear a voice speaking in the neighbourhood of Bethany on a dark and stormy day, another day of sorrow and mystery. The words uttered by that voice were not in the nature of a question, casting a gleam of light, but a great affirmation, creating the break of the day of perfect light. " He that believeth on Me, though he die, yet shall he live."

Job's consciousness of human life, based upon the experience of the hour, was expressed in these words :

> " Man that is born of a woman
> Is of few days, and full of trouble.
> He cometh forth like a flower, and is cut down ;
> He fleeth also as a shadow, and continueth not."

And as later he said :

> " For there is hope of a tree, if it be cut down, that it will sprout again."

Thus Job declared that as he saw things, in the darkness of his experience, there was more hope for a tree than for a man. The tree cut down, sprouts again. Though there is an appearance of death, the scent of water will cause the tender branch to bud out of the old root, for life is still there.

> " But man dieth, and wasteth away ;
> Yea, man giveth up the ghost, and where is he ? "

This is a great poetic interpretation of massed human thinking. We are all given thus to think of life, even though it may be we have never put the thinking into words as Job did. When he uttered these words, he was in such circumstances as made him careless of anything merely conventional. He was baring his soul. He was expressing what he felt. Of course he was viewing his life on the side of the physical. Yet as he did so, there was a sudden recognition that he was more than dust. He realized that dying meant giving up the spirit. Looking out into the dark void he said :

> " Yea, man giveth up the spirit, and where
>   is he ? . . .
> So man lieth down and riseth not ;
> Till the heavens be no more, they shall
>   not awake,
> Nor be roused out of their sleep."

Then he cried :

> " If a man die, shall he live ? "

I repeat, that is the common human outlook. It is what men are saying to-day, so far as the sense of the meaning of death is concerned.

Often, also, in the midst of such thinking, Job's question arises. Alas! too often it would seem as though men do not ask that question. They continue, too largely without giving any attention to the spiritual fact. They go on eating and drinking, living wholly on the plane of the physical. Job, however, was now stripped of all earthly supports, and was facing the nakedness of his own being. When men get there, they are almost coerced into Job's inquiry in some form. After all, what is life? Is it worth while? It began beautifully, like a flower opening, but it is soon to be cut off.

We need carefully to observe the real meaning of Job's question. In our translations we have introduced a word " again." This is not what Job asked. It was not an inquiry as to whether a dead man should come back to life; but whether a man dead so far as the physical is concerned, still lives. If a man die, if the flower is cut off, is that man still alive? The question has not to do with a possible return to life, but is concerned with the idea of the continuity of life beyond what men call death.

All this might be put in another form. Job

suddenly said within himself, Is life after all something more than the present experience of it ?   Can it be that what we call death is only a change ?   If a man die, is he still living ?

The question in itself is a revelation of the consciousness of the need for more time and space for the realization of life than the span of earthly life can afford.   In effect Job said, If I could be sure that this life was not all, that the thing called death is but a process through which man passes, then the present, however full of suffering, would be bearable. I could stand up against all the bludgeonings of fate.   I could bear anything if I thought I should still live, when men said I was dead.

This was the cry of a human being for more time and space for the interpretation of life. It was only a question, a sob, a sigh ; only a suggestion ; and the gleam faded, and Job passed back into the gloom.

That is the constant cry of humanity.   Max Müller long ago said that if we only listened carefully enough we could hear universally :

> " A groaning of the spirit, a struggle to conceive the inconceivable, to utter the unutterable, a longing after the Infinite."

Max Müller said that that was religion. Personally I should say that it demonstrates the capacity for religion. All that was condensed in Job's inquiry. Confronting death, he asked his question. The view of death was and is a dark one. In spite of much that has been said, there is no bright view of death. The New Testament never refers to death in that way. It distinctly calls it an enemy. " The last enemy that shall be destroyed is death."

It is perfectly true that the answer of Jesus has transfigured the sackcloth. We may address death triumphantly as Bishop Taylor did :

" Death, the old serpent's son,
    Thou hadst a sting once, like thy sire,
    That carried hell and ever-burning fire ;
  But those black days are done ;
  Thy foolish spite buried thy sting
    In the profound and wide
    Wound of our Saviour's side ;
  And now thou art become a tame and harmless
      thing ;
    A thing we dare not fear,
    Since we hear
  That our triumphant God, to punish thee
  For the affront thou didst Him on the tree
    Hath snatched the keys of hell out of thy hand,
    And made thee stand
  A porter at the gate of life, thy mortal enemy."

To say that, however, is somewhat to run ahead of the argument of our meditation to the second part thereof. To return for a moment to this outlook on death, man does not want to die, because he is conscious that his life is so big that it cannot find full interpretation in the brief span of its earthly course. In the realm of investigation, the student, the scholar who for perhaps fifty years and more has pursued some line of investigation, and has by no means reached finality, passes away. He passes when he is more fitted for work than he has ever been before. Nothing is completed. In olden time, and perhaps still in many of our cemeteries, they erected over the dust of some departed being as a monument, a broken column. These are very suggestive as indicating the fact of the incompleteness of life. It is true that often across the broken-off apex, a garland of flowers was carved: That, too, was full of beautiful suggestiveness. Job, when he asked his question, saw the broken column with no garland of flowers. For a moment he wistfully wondered, Is this all ? This prosperity merging into penury, this anguish and agony of unsolved problems, and of his friends' utter misunderstanding ; is this indeed the end ?

" If a man die, shall he live ? "

Are there other dimensions ? Is there still more time and space ?

Now the question arises, is there an answer to that inquiry ? Certainly there is none in the Book of Job. When presently God came to deal with Job, He uttered no explanation of his pain, did not answer any question that had been asked. What He did was to make His own glory pass before the man ; and it is significant that when He did so, Job had no other question to ask. He became willing to postpone them.

We should not be warranted in saying that there was no positive conviction in the souls of any of these Old Testament men of the fact of immortality. But it may be affirmed that in the whole of the Old Testament Scriptures nothing is to be found that definitely and finally proves it. There are gleams, suggestions, implicates, and deductions, all the way through ; but nothing authoritative. The answer to Job's question came with full and final authority in Jesus. This is what Paul meant when writing to Timothy he said, clustering the titles of our Lord into a great order, " Our Saviour Jesus Christ abolished death, and brought life and immortality to light through the Gospel." In passing we may remind ourselves that the word "immortality" has been rendered more accurately by our revisers "incorruption." In his first letter to Timothy Paul declared that " God . . . only hath immortality," being the word *athanasia*, which means eternal deathlessness. Here he declared that Jesus brought life and *aphtharsia* to light. *Aphtharsia* merely refers to a quality of life which lacks any element tending to decay or corruption. Further let it be noted that Paul does not say that our Lord through the Gospel created life and incorruption ; but that He brought them to light. That is, He brought into clear visibility facts that were in existence. He brought the full and final answer to Job's question. We may put the thing quite bluntly thus. Job said, " If a man die, shall he live ? " Said Jesus, Yes, " he that believeth on Me, though he die, yet shall he live."

Let us pause for a moment to look at the

circumstances under which these words of our Lord were uttered. Lazarus was dead. The great human question applied to him would be, Where is he? Does he still live? Those standing around were gazing at a dead body, and if they attempted to peer into the gloom there was no ray of light. It was then that Jesus said to Martha, "Thy brother shall rise again." When with honesty she declared her belief in resurrection, He added, "I am the Resurrection and the Life," and added, "he that believeth on Me, though he die, yet shall he live." These words then did not refer to resurrection, although that also had been declared. They affirmed his continued life beyond what men look upon as death.

Then we are halted by the words, "He that believeth on Me," and find ourselves confronted by a situation which compels us to recognize that the Speaker was more than Man. This was the very language of God. The man who lives his life in fellowship with God never dies. To Job, or those in his case, the affirmation declares that there is more room than can be found in the dust-heap where they scrape themselves with potsherds for very agony.

There is more time than the turning sand-glass indicates.

We are living in the full light of this revelation, and to live there is to be assured that all physical death is incidental. Necessarily this fact has many applications. To begin with one, which perhaps is of minor importance, it at least implicates the fact of the recognition of our loved ones in the Life that lies beyond. How constantly people are asking questions in that realm. There comes to me a simple memory from the days when I was a lad about thirteen years of age. My father had been preaching, and I was standing by his side afterwards, when a good woman came to him, and said, " Mr. Morgan, do you expect to know your loved ones in heaven ? " He had a brusquerie of manner oftentimes, and his reply to her may have that element in it, but I have never lost the impression it made upon me. He said, " My good woman, do you expect I shall be a bigger fool in heaven than here ? " It was the answer of a man who believed that beyond death is life, and intelligent life.

In the realm of conscious personality this

word of Jesus emphasizes the greatness of being, the splendour of individuality. To exist is magnificent, so magnificent that it is impossible to put the measurement of threescore years and ten upon life. The real meaning of life lies out beyond that. There is to be ample time and space for the complete interpretation and realization of what God meant when He gave us being. That puts an entirely different complexion upon the days that, hurrying on, bear us towards the end of the earthly pilgrimage. The now is ever leading to the then. Every passing hour is linked with the undying ages.

Of course, that gives supreme value to these passing days. We may not, indeed, we cannot, see their full meaning as they pass. It is impossible to know the reason of to-day's experiences. The ultimate meaning of life lies out beyond what men call death. It was this conception that inspired Frances Ridley Havergal when she sang :

> " Light after darkness,
>   Gain after loss,
>   Strength after weakness,
>   Crown after cross ;

> Sweet after bitter,
> Hope after fears,
> Home after wandering,
> Praise after tears."

Out of darkness light will come ; out of the loss of time the gain of eternity ; out of the weakness of the hour the strength that abides ; out of the cross is coming the crown ; out of the bitter comes the sweet ; fear ends in hope that never dies ; all wandering is leading Home ; and tears, encircled by the rainbow of love, will produce the praise that surrounds the rainbow-girdled Throne.

Yes, if a man dies, he lives, if he believes in Him through Whom God is revealed, and by Whom man passes into fellowship with God. D. L. Moody once said : " Some fine morning you will see in the newspapers, D. L. Moody is dead. Don't you believe it. I shall be more alive that morning than ever before ! "

IV

THE WITNESS IN HEAVEN

" Even now, behold, my witness is in heaven,
And He that voucheth for me is on high."—JOB xvi. 19.

" For Christ entered . . . into heaven itself, now to
appear before . . . God for us."—HEBREWS ix. 24.

IN these two passages we have another great
cry of Job, and the answer to it found in Jesus.
These particular words of Job occur in the
second cycle of the controversy between him
and his friends. In the first cycle Eliphaz,
Bildad, and Zophar all addressed him, attempting to account for his suffering in one way,
declaring that it must be the result of personal
sin. Job had hotly protested against the in-
accuracy of their findings. Now in his second
address Eliphaz had reiterated the same philosophy more vigorously than at the first. The
whole of Eliphaz's speech may be summarized
as a declaration that it is only the wicked who
suffer. It is, of course, perfectly true that the
wicked do suffer, but it is by no means all the

truth. Again Job angrily reaffirmed his innocence. A sentence or two from the beginning
of his answer will reveal its scorn :

> " I have heard many such things ;
> Miserable comforters are ye all,
> Shall vain words have an end ? "

By which he meant, Are you going to say the
same thing again ? Will you never cease ?
Job was angry because he knew they were
wrong, knew that his suffering was not the
result of his own sin. Thus we hear him
reaffirming his innocence :

> " Although there is no violence in my
>   hands,
> And my prayer is pure."

In the midst of his angry reply, and his earnest
protestations of innocence, and the outpouring
of his soul in anguish, suddenly he said :

> " Even now, behold, my witness is in
>   heaven,
> And He that voucheth for me is on high."

In these words he gave utterance to a great
conviction. Evidently it was a sudden ejacula-
tion. It would appear to have been as un-

expected to Job as to those who listened to
him. Yet it did express a conviction ; and in
the midst of turmoil, anguish, and anger, he
gave utterance to it. The word " Behold "
indicates the arresting nature of the thing he
said. " Even now," amid the misunderstanding
of friends, in the presence of his own bewilder-
ment, he was conscious that there was One
Who knew, and Who was able to attest the
truth.

Immediately following upon the exclamation,
he declared that his trouble was that he could
not reach that One, or that the One thus
referred to did not appear to be acting on His
behalf. He cried :

> " My friends scorn me ;
>> But mine eye poureth out tears unto
>> God ;
>> That He would maintain the right of a
>> man with God."

If we can imaginatively come into the experience and consciousness of Job, we shall understand all he said. He found himself in the
midst of turmoil, filled with anguish, facing the
tragedy of listening to good men, true men,

fine men, talking to him about his experiences, while yet ignorant of the facts concerning him. This great cry was uttered in close connection with a passionate appeal.

As we look back on Job's experience at this time in the light of subsequent events and of fuller revelation, we are conscious that Job was wrong. Not in his conviction concerning his witness in heaven, but in his opinion that God was not acting for him. We are quite prepared to admit the truth of the lines :

> " Thrice blest is he to whom is given
>   The instinct that can tell
> That God is on the field, when He
>   Is most invisible."

We realize that God is on the field, and that there He is governing actively. But we also have known, sooner or later, what it is to pass through experiences when it seemed to us that He was doing nothing. That was Job's experience at the moment. Nevertheless behind all the turmoil of his intellectual and emotional nature he had, and gave utterance to, this word of conviction. Let us therefore consider the conviction thus expressed, and how it has received ratification and interpretation in Jesus.

In considering the cry of Job we notice that he made an affirmation of a twofold nature. The first declared, " My witness is in heaven." By " witness " he intended a watcher, who knows, and knows all. He was surrounded by men who were perfectly honest, and were his friends, but who failed in what they were saying to him, because they did not know all. They thought they did. They were endeavouring to account for the experiences of a man by a partial and incomplete philosophy. In the midst of the suffering of this misunderstanding, he declared his conviction that there was One in heaven watching, understanding, knowing all.

Then repeating the same truth in a slightly different form, with perhaps a changed application, he said,

" And He that voucheth for me is on high."

The King James Version rendered that, " My record is on high," which was an entirely misleading translation. The Hebrew word there does not mean a record. Permissibly it might be rendered " my Recorder," that is, the One Who sees all, knows all, and Whose findings are according to this knowledge ; the One able to vouch for him, or bear witness to the truth concerning him.

Thus we see a man in the dust, a man in agony, a man surrounded by the clamour of people who meant well, but who did not understand him. Suddenly his soul leapt beyond the bounds of time and space and the chatter of ignorance. He said, There is a Watcher Who knows. There is a Recorder Whose findings are according to perfect knowledge. It was the consciousness of the ultimate Tribunal, " Heaven," above the earth, " on high," beyond which there is no appeal.

It is quite true that Job immediately recoiled from his own affirmation, and spoke of his sorrow and his anguish, and the sense that filled him at the moment that he could not reach this Watcher and Voucher.   There are senses in which this cry revealed human consciousness of need at its deepest ; which is that of an ultimate court of appeal and judgment, uninfluenced by incomplete knowledge and the deceits of appearances.   Such a court cannot be found on the earth level.   It is perfectly true that our friends give us tender and kindly judgments, but they cannot do so upon the basis of perfect knowledge, and appearances will constantly deceive them. These friends of Job were all good men, meaning well, but their knowledge was incomplete, and what they saw misled them, because their philosophy was imperfect. The cry of Job revealed a conviction that there is a court where knowledge is not incomplete, and where the appearances of the passing hour cannot deceive. His outburst was that of conviction that the only hope of justice is that the Judge Himself should be the Advocate ; and to this the deepest in human consciousness ever responds. How perpetually we find ourselves in circumstances where we passionately desire to escape from human judgments, based upon imperfect knowledge. Perhaps no day passes in which false judgments are not formed, which nevertheless may be perfectly sincere.

We now turn to the New Testament and to the letter to the Hebrews. In order to understand our selection therefrom, we must remind ourselves of the general purpose and value of the letter. Its background is that of the Hebrew system of nationality and religion.

The Hebrew nation, according to the Divine intention, was a Theocracy, and to this all its religious ceremonial was intended to bear perpetual witness. If with the simplicity of children we call to mind the Biblical account of the camp, we shall be helped. The place of the Tabernacle was at the centre of the national life, and around it the varied tribes encamped, underneath their respective banners. At the centre of all the courts of the place of worship was the Holy place, and the Holy of Holies. The truth thus illustrated and insisted upon was that at the centre of all life, is God ; and that human conditions of life, and human life itself, can only realize their meaning and possibility as they revolve around that centre, under that government.

The writer of the letter to the Hebrews from beginning to end was showing that the symbolism has passed away, because everything that was symbolized had come into practical and historic fulfilment in Christ. In the particular passage from which the words we are considering were taken, the writer declares that " Christ hath not entered into the holy place made with hands." That is to say, the old economy has passed away, and the reason for its passing is found in the fact that " He hath entered into heaven itself, to appear in the presence of God for us."

Here again the central facts of life are recognized, heaven and God ; and the declaration is made that Christ has entered heaven and has appeared in the presence of God for us. Thus the argument of the writer is that there is now One Who is God in His own nature and yet is actually Man, Who stands in the presence of God, knowing perfectly, and He does so on our behalf. He stands before God, vindicating the sinner. He has become the Witness, by the mystery of His personality in human history, and of the work accomplished through that mystery. He came into human history supernaturally, lived on the earthly level, triumphing over all sin and earthly limitation ; and then passed beyond the sight of earth-bound vision, but remaining, a living personality, this same Jesus. All that Job had felt the need of, and avowed his conviction concerning, in the process of human history, had come into historic visibility. Applying it to ourselves we may say Christ has entered in, and there is our

Witness, our Recorder. He is the One Who perfectly knows, and therefore is able prevailingly to mediate.

In every human life the findings of God are the supreme things. That is, of course, equally true concerning the widest outlook on human nature and human history. For the moment let us apply it to individual human life. There is a story which has often been told, but is of value in this connection. It concerns Jowett at the time that he was Master of Balliol in Oxford. He was a great man in every way and characterized by rapier-like wit. One day at a dinner, a lady, hoping to draw some clever response from him, said to him, " Dr. Jowett, we would like to know what is your opinion of God." The Master's aspect at once became stern, and he said, " Madam, I should think it a great impertinence were I to express my opinion about God. The only constant anxiety of my life is to know what is God's opinion of me."

And in the last analysis, that is the one thing that is important. Job felt his need of that judgment and of a declaration concerning it. He was conscious of his own innocence, but he could not prove it to the satisfaction of men. One thing to him was a certainty. For the passing moment, even though the conviction seems to have been dimmed afterwards, it was that there was One knowing all the facts concerning him, and so able to form right judgments concerning him.

If we are conscious of fear in the presence of the conviction of this knowledge of God, it is well that we ask ourselves why are we afraid? If we do this, we shall find that our fear is the result of His holiness, and the consciousness that there is something in our lives out of harmony with that holiness.

This is the point at which the final comfort of the conviction of this ultimate Tribunal is found in the Person of Jesus. If our fear is created by our own moral failure, we remember that it is at that point that Christ begins to deal with us. He Who entered within the veil, Who passed into the presence of God, there to appear for us, came there by the way of the Cross. Let the holy and inspired language of Scripture be retained. He " entered by His own blood." He Who stands in the presence of God as my Witness, bears the scars that tell of suffering unto death, and testify that He is the Redeemer.

Sin being dealt with, He stands in the presence of God, my Witness, representing me as the Saviour. To Him I may go at all times for judgment, passing all others by, careless in the last analysis of all other opinion, which may be mistaken through lack of knowledge, through the deceit of appearances. In Browning's great poem on Saul, he said :

> " 'Tis the weakness in strength, that I cry for ! my flesh, that I seek
> In the Godhead ! I seek and I find it. O Saul, it shall be
> A Face like my face that receives thee ; a Man like to me
> Thou shalt love and be loved by, for ever ; a Hand like this hand
> Shall throw open the gates of new life to thee ! See the Christ stand ! "

V

THE LIVING REDEEMER

" I know that my Redeemer liveth."—JOB xix. 25.
" He ever liveth to make intercession."—HEBREWS vii. 25.

THESE words of Job are found in the second
cycle of his controversy with his friends, and
are contained in his answer to Bildad. Bildad,
under varying figures of speech, had described
the sufferings of Job, and by describing them
had added to them. He had declared that
such sufferings were only found in the dwellings
of wickedness, the implicate being that wickedness, somewhere in the life of Job, was the
reason of his sufferings. That was the persistent
argument of his friends. Job, angry and
scornful, replied, declaring that he knew his
afflictions were from God, and saying that these
men had no right to add to them. His reply
as a whole was a definite denial of the charge
thus implicitly made against him. In the

midst of that reply, and out of the deep
darkness in which Job found himself, there
suddenly broke this great cry, this affirmation shining as a gleam of light. It was only
transient. The next sentences show that he
sank back at once into the gloom. But for
the moment this remarkable gleam shone
forth.

He had declared previously that his Witness
was in heaven, and his Recorder on high ; but
in this he went still further, and gave his
Witness the name of Redeemer.

The beauty of these words is self-evident.
It is impossible for us to read them without
being conscious of the final interpretation of
them in Christ. Let us however, for the
moment, remember that the profoundest values
of them Job could not have realized. These
values were only brought into clear light by the
Incarnation. Nevertheless the cry came out
of his essential spirit life. Suddenly amid the
darkness, and overwhelmed by the sorrows of
the hour, Job seems to have caught the music
of eternal things, as it swept across the strings
which seemed to be broken by suffering. It is
as though the personality of Job was like an

æolian harp across which the wind sweeps, making music. If he had, and could have, no complete sense of the historic fulfilment of the thing he said, nevertheless the great underlying eternal truth was recognized ; and of it Job had, momentarily at least, a consciousness as he broke out into these wonderful words :

> " I know that my Redeemer liveth,
>> And that He shall stand up at the last upon the earth ;
>> And after my skin hath been thus destroyed,
>> Yet from my flesh shall I see God ;
>> Whom I shall see for myself,
>> And mine eyes shall behold, and not another."

Then the light faded immediately, and the next sentence ran :

> " My reins are consumed within me."

Let us then consider the affirmation of Job, attempting to understand it, as to what it meant to him ; and then turn to find the full interpretation and realization in Jesus.

The words, "My Redeemer" have a fulness of meaning to us which can only be interpreted in the incarnate Son of God. It is important that we should understand what the word meant as Job uttered it. The Hebrew word is the word "Goel," which is found scattered across the pages of the Old Testament Literature. To these people the "Goel" was the nearest and next of kin, whose duty it was to undertake the cause of another in case of need. We find most about the "Goel" in the Book of Ruth, where we have an illustration of the activity of such an one. We may summarize by saying that the "Goel" stood for another to defend his cause, to avenge wrongs done to him, and so to acquit him of all charges laid against him. In that sense Job said, "I know that my Redeemer liveth." The statement did not merely mean that his Redeemer existed. It is as though Job had said, 'Even though I die, He lives.' His declaration proved that in the midst of his agony for a moment at least, he was convinced that while there was no one to stand for him in life, all his friends having misunderstood him, all his acquaintances having left him, he yet had a Kinsman Who was his Advocate, his Avenger, the One through Whom he would be acquitted.

In interpretation he ran on, affirming that this Redeemer would yet stand upon the earth, that is, upon the dust. The figure is entirely Eastern, and affirmed his conviction that somewhere in the future, if not at the moment, his " Goel " would stand as a Witness to his integrity.

All this is emphasized, as continuing, he said :

> " Yet from my flesh shall I see God ;
> Whom I shall see for myself,
> And mine eyes shall behold, and not
> another."

This was a consciousness, not merely of the fact of the existence of the Vindicator, but a conviction that he himself would see Him. At this point a question arises, which has caused some difficulty. What was the real meaning of that word " from," in the phrase, " from my flesh " ? There are those who hold that it means away from the flesh ; whereas there are those who understand it to mean, being

still present in the flesh. The language of
Rosalind in Shakespeare, " I thought it well
to write from my home," certainly meant that
she was away from home ; but it may be
equally true when writing a letter to say you
write from your home and mean that you are
at home when you are writing. Whether Job
was then thinking of his existence as a spirit
beyond the death of his body ; or whether he
was affirming a belief in resurrection, cannot
be dogmatically decided. The one certain
thing, however, is that he was conscious of
the continuity of his personality beyond what
we call death. There we have reached the
revelation of the greatness of his affirmation.
Suddenly, for a passing moment, there came
to this stricken man the widest outlook, in-
cluding all the truth concerning God and himself : the fact of the inter-relationship of the
present with the future.

Continuing, he declared on the basis of that
conviction, that his Vindicator, his " Goel,"
would not only stand for him, but that he would
see God. The very Cimmerian gloom in which
Job was then living, and which seems to
have settled back upon him immediately

afterwards, serves to make the more remarkable this declaration that he found in
God, One committed to him as a Redeemer.
In a previous meditation we heard him ask
the question, "If a man die, shall he
live?" Here for a moment he had passed
beyond the question, and was affirming that
beyond death he himself would live; and
moreover, would see God, and see Him as
his Redeemer.

The question which arises is as to whether
Job was right in that moment of illumination.
Were the things that he saw true? I am not
asking were they to become true in the future.
Were they then true? The answer is of course
found in the Incarnation. The Incarnation
originated nothing other than complete revelation. When God became flesh in Jesus He
did not come nearer to human nature than He
had ever been; but He came into visibility.
By that coming there was revealed the fact
that what Job had said was literally true.
Here we find the value of the words of the
writer of the letter to the Hebrews, " He is
able to save to the uttermost them that come
unto God through Him, for He ever liveth to

make intercession for us." He is the " Goel," pleading our cause, and undertaking for us in every way.

It is an arresting fact that this statement in the letter to the Hebrews is found in close connection, and indeed is the culminating statement of the writer's references to Melchizedek. This Melchizedek is only referred to twice in Old Testament Literature : once in the history of Abraham, and once in a great Hebrew song. The writer of this letter to the Hebrews now takes hold of that Person, and declares that Jesus is a Priest of that order ; and ultimately affirms that He " ever liveth to make intercession."

In Him therefore we find the complete fulfilment of what dawned upon Job in the midst of the darkness, as the shining of a light of hope and confidence. The One Who ever lives came into our earthly life, stood upon the dust for us, and argued our case on the earth level. By that unveiling we are brought to an understanding of how He for ever represents us, and argues our case in the high courts of heaven.

To return to our question : Was Job right ?

Or was the thing that he saw a mirage of the desert, having no substance and no value? The answer to the inquiry is given, as we have said, in Jesus. When Job, amid the desolation, declared that he had a " Goel " living and active, he was uttering a profound truth, the truth that in God, man has his Redeemer in all the fullest senses of that great word. It was a spiritual apprehension of an abiding fact, which fact came into clear shining when God was manifest in flesh. Jean Ingelow had a glimpse into the heart of the truth when she sang :

> " And didst Thou love the race that loved not Thee ?
> And didst Thou take to heaven a human brow ?
> Dost plead with man's voice by the marvellous sea ?
> Art Thou his Kinsman now ?
>
> O God, O Kinsman loved, but not enough,
> O Man with eyes majestic after death,
> Whose feet have toiled along our pathways rough,
> Whose lips drawn human breath."

He ever liveth, our " Goel," our Kinsman Redeemer, vindicating us, in spite of our sin, by His redeeming work, filling to the full all the suggestiveness of the word that Job employed ; and indeed, more than filling it. Job throughout was arguing that he was not suffering for his sin, and he was right in so doing ; but there are those who are suffering directly on account of their sin. To them also the great word applies in the Divine purpose and accomplishment ; for as a Kinsman He takes their sin, and so deals with it that they may be justified. This One " ever liveth to make intercession for us."

VI

THE QUEST FOR GOD

" Oh that I knew where I might find Him ! "—Job xxiii. 3.
" He that hath seen Me hath seen the Father."—John xiv. 9.

THESE words of Job are found in the third and final cycle of his controversy with his friends. Eliphaz had delivered his last speech. It was briefer than his earlier ones, and was direct, blunt, and even brutal. Maintaining his position that Job's sufferings must be the result of Job's sins, he described the kind of sins which would be likely to produce such sufferings ; and by implication attributed them to Job, though he had no evidence. It was all speculative, and entirely false. His speech ended with advice to Job in a passage of great beauty, the first sentence of which expressed the whole of its appeal :

" Acquaint now thyself with Him."

In his reply, Job ignored the charges which

had been brought against him, and replied to
the advice thus tendered. He tacitly admitted
the excellence of the advice, but immediately,
in the words we are considering, revealed the
difficulty of which he was conscious. Bluntly
Eliphaz had said, Get to know God, and all
will be peace. Job replied in effect, That is
the difficulty. How am I going to do it?
And in these actual words, " Oh that I knew
where I might find Him!" It is one thing to
tell a man to acquaint himself with God, but
quite another to show him how he is to do it.

" Oh that I knew where I might find Him!"

That was the language of a man who had
underlying convictions about God. It is con-
ceivable that such a question might be asked
flippantly. Yes, it is evidently possible for a
man of brilliant intellect to write the story of
a Black Girl's search for God with a knobkerry;
but a story characterized by such lack of
seriousness is hardly worth attention. Job's
query was not in that spirit. The context
shows how conscious he was of the fact and
presence of God. He knew He was at work,
but declared that He was hiding Himself.

Moreover, he was convinced that if he could find Him, " He would give heed " unto him ; and that " the upright might reason with Him." Notwithstanding this double conviction of the fact of God, and of the justice of God, his difficulty was that he could not reach Him. In language of strange poetical beauty, and yet lucid declaration, he described his quest after God. He said, " I go forward, but He is not there. I go backward, but I cannot perceive Him." I am conscious that He is at work, and I turn to the left, but cannot behold Him. He is on the right hand ; I know He is there, but He is in hiding, and I cannot see Him. On the earthly level he turned in every direction, forward and backward, to the left and to the right. An old Puritan writer quaintly observed, in commenting on this, " Job, you have gone forward and backward, and you have looked to the left and you have looked to the right. Why don't you try looking up ? " The comment is suggestive, but Job would still have said he could not reach Him.

That is an abiding human consciousness when men seek for God on the earth level. They may be perfectly sincere. Their search,

like that of Job, may be the result of pressure
and tribulation and suffering ; or it may be
the search of the intellect for the solution of
the riddle of the universe. God is not denied ;
nay, there may be conviction that He is ; but
He cannot thus be found. Man cannot make
contact with God by any action which is earth-
bound. On a low level of illustration, we may
refer to people who tell us that they find God
in Nature, and therefore have no need for the
activities of worship. This is not true. They
may see the evidences of God in Nature, for
all creation is the vesture of Deity, wrought
in beauty, and radiant with glory ; but God
is never found in Nature in such a way as to
satisfy the deepest necessity of human life.

This cry :

" Oh that I knew where I might find Him! "

is ultimately a revelation of the necessity for
some special revelation of God to the spiritual
side of the nature of man. In an earlier cycle
of the controversy Zophar had said to Job :

" Can'st thou by searching find out God ? "

Now when his friend Eliphaz advises Job to

acquaint himself with God, Job in his answer is but ratifying the difficulty as expressed in the earlier question of Zophar.

From this revelation of human necessity, as expressed in the cry of Job, we turn to the answer of Jesus. Many intervening centuries had run their course, and we find ourselves in an upper room with a group of men of our own humanity, men who have also known this desire of the spiritual life for God. In the midst of them there was One, a Man of their humanity, looking with human eyes at them, as they are looking at Him. Nevertheless, He is the One in Whom all the eternal came into visibility. That is the meaning of the Incarnation. It was not the beginning of anything new in the eternal facts, but the shining forth of these facts upon human life. In this company there sat a quiet man, with a Greek name ; and I hear him say exactly what Job said, if in other words, " Show us the Father, and it sufficeth us."

Much has been written about what Philip really meant. It has been suggested that he was asking for some such outshining as had been given to Moses ; that he was requesting a supernatural manifestation. I do not think anything is gained by discussing this matter. The one certain thing is that Philip was seeking some vision which would certify God to his soul. Again it was an elemental cry of humanity in the measure in which humanity has lost its consciousness of God.

To that cry the answer of Jesus was given in a clear, unequivocal declaration, " He that hath seen Me hath seen the Father."

That affirmation might be considered in many ways. I choose one only. Let us go back to Philip. When Jesus said to him, " Have I been so long time with you, and dost thou not know Me, Philip ? he that hath seen Me hath seen the Father," He was asking Philip to look back over the period in which he had been with Him. Philip was one of the first disciples, and he had been with Jesus through the whole period of His public ministry. We have the account of four occasions in which he is seen in personal contact with Him.

The first was when Jesus sought him at the beginning, " Jesus findeth Philip, and saith

unto him, Come and travel with Me." That is
when he first saw Him. " He that hath seen
Me."

Then much later in the course of our Lord's
ministry, when the multitudes were thronging
upon Him, and He was moved with compassion,
it was to Philip that He talked. To him He
said, " Whence are we to buy bread, that these
may eat ? " He was not asking Philip for
information, for John says, " This He said to
prove him, for He Himself knew what He
would do." The issue was that Philip saw
Him that day feed the multitude. " He that
hath seen Me."

Then Philip was the man to whom the Greeks
came with their request, " Sir, we would see
Jesus." After consultation with Andrew, they
came and told the Lord. Philip listened to
that marvellous answer of Jesus, beginning with
the declaration, " The hour is come that the
Son of man should be glorified. Verily, verily,
I say unto you, Except a grain of wheat fall
into the earth and die, it abideth by itself
alone ; but if it die, it beareth much fruit " ;
and continuing presently He cried, " Now is
My soul troubled " ; and later, " Now is the

judgment of this world." Of course the whole
of this answer should be read. These sentences
are sufficient to show that our Lord was facing
His Cross, and in spite of His experience of
sorrow, saw through to its triumph. Philip
was watching Him then. " He that hath seen
Me."

Now in the Upper Room, certainly not long
after this revelation at the coming of the
Greeks, he had seen Jesus gird Himself with a
towel, and bend in the attitude of a slave, and
wash his feet. Thus he had seen Him. " He
that hath seen Me."

Now He said, " Dost thou not know Me,
Philip ? he that hath seen Me hath seen the
Father." In all these things the Father was
seen, seeking the man, meeting the hunger of
the crowd physically, and lifting the action
into the realm of the spiritual in teaching ;
finally facing and moving towards the infinite
mystery of pain through which humanity could
be ransomed and redeemed ; bending until He
took the place of a bond-slave, serving a group
of men who believed in Him.

After uttering these things He gave Philip
proofs of the claim He had made, declaring

that the words He uttered were from the Father, and the works He did were the works of the Father.

At this point it may be well to remind ourselves that all through the revelation of our Lord found in this Gospel according to John, the words and the works are in mind, and always the words are treated as supreme ; and the fact is emphasized that these were from God, and that the works were also the works of God. He then appealed to Philip and the rest in the words, " Believe Me . . . or else believe Me for the very works' sake." The first line of proof was Himself. " Believe Me " was a call to the consideration of His personality. " Or else," that is, if you cannot rise to the higher level of the understanding of My personality, then " believe Me for the very works' sake."

This challenge is an abiding one. If we will consider the Man Jesus, as He is revealed in the New Testament, we are inevitably brought face to face with the fact that through the human, something other than the human is for ever shining round about us. Let us take up the New Testament with its presentation of the Person of our Lord, in these Gospel narratives, and open it at any point, and then carefully look at Him. We may find Him in Bethesda's porches among the derelicts. We may find Him with the children in His arms. We may find Him in the midst of the rulers with a sin-smirched woman in the midst of a watching crowd. Wherever we find Him—if I may adopt a mathematical method—let us project the lines from Him into infinitude, and we shall find we are seeing God.

We may see Him on a day when His eyes are flaming with fire, and His words are hot as the burnings of Gehenna against hyprocrisy. That is God. We may see Him when those selfsame eyes are bedewed with tears. Twice over we so see Him. Lazarus was dead. Martha and Mary were in trouble. Jesus wept. That is God. That is how God feels when we are broken-hearted in the presence of the death of our loved ones. Again we see Him with heaving breast, sobbing in His grief. Jerusalem was doomed, but His heart was breaking as He pronounced the sentence. That is God.

John, in the prologue of his Gospel, declares

"We beheld His glory, glory as of the only begotten from the Father, full of grace and truth."

Thus, to the cry of humanity,

> " Oh that I knew where I might find Him! "
> " Show us the Father and it sufficeth us " ;

the answer is full and final, " He that hath seen Me hath seen the Father." On an earlier occasion our Lord had said, " All things have been delivered unto Me of My Father; and no one knoweth the Son, save the Father; neither doth any know the Father save the Son, and he to whomsoever the Son willeth to reveal Him." In connection with that affirmation He uttered His great call, " Come unto Me . . . and I will give you rest." On this same occasion He said, " No one cometh unto the Father, but by Me." He answers the quest of the soul after God, and so brings it to the place of perfect rest.

The question may still be asked by honest souls, How are we to know that these things that Jesus is reported to have said are so ? In an earlier period of His ministry He had uttered the revealing words, " If any man willeth to do His will, he shall know of the teaching, whether it be of God." He thus declared that there must be first of all a supreme determination to do the will of God ; and then that the proof that He spoke from God would be found. When there was obedience, there would come the demonstration which would satisfy the soul that the things spoken were of God. The man who wills to do the will of God is the man whose moral intention is what it ought to be, for the will of God is always that of holiness. I do not say moral achievement. Our Lord did not say that if men would do the will of God they would understand ; but if they willed to do it.

Merely intellectual interest will never find God, even in Jesus. Job and Philip were seeking God, because they were convinced of His government and His justice. They were therefore ready for revelation. Revelation did come to Job subsequently partially, but never fully. To Philip it was given in all its fulness in the Person of our Lord.

Thus, the way in which the human soul can find the answer to its quest for God is revealed.

When spiritual intention harmonizes with the universal law of righteousness, spiritual intelligence will discover that God was in Christ. " He that hath seen Me hath seen the Father."

VII

THE CHALLENGE TO GOD

" Oh that I had One to hear me ! . . .
   And that I had the indictment which mine Adversary
hath written ! "—JOB xxxi. 35.

" Ye are come . . . to God the Judge of all . . . and to
Jesus the Mediator."—HEBREWS xii. 22–24.

In these words of Job we have his last appeal,
and it is in the nature of a direct challenge to
God.

The cycles of controversy with his friends
were now over. In this third and last, Eliphaz
and Bildad had spoken, and Job had answered.
Zophar had nothing to say. Evidently after a
pause Job uttered his last speech. In it he
first surveyed his past prosperity and adversity,
and claimed that he had just cause for all his
complaining.

In this final cycle Eliphaz and Bildad had
maintained their contention that the sufferings
of Job must be evidence of his sin. To this
Job replied by once more reaffirming his inno-

cence, and in these words uttered his challenge. All the way through he had been misunderstood by men, and felt that he could not make contact with God. To put it quite bluntly, he seems to have felt at this point that God was not playing the game. I have said that is a blunt statement, but it does represent a common human experience in hours when the soul is overwhelmed with sorrow, which seems to have neither reason nor explanation.

The language of Job was judicial, that is to say, the appeal was based upon processes in a court of law. The word " adversary " here is a purely legal one, and we might render it in our present terminology " a prosecutor." It refers to one conducting the case against a defendant. In the thinking of Job, God was conceived of as the Adversary in that sense, and himself as defendant. In the ancient courts of law two things were always demanded : first, the statement by the prosecutor of the charge preferred ; and secondly, the statement of the defendant in rebuttal of the charge. The order of procedure was that the prosecutor first states his case, and then the defendant his.

The position of Job, as revealed in this exclamation, was that he had never had the case against him stated by his Adversary, but that he had prepared his defence. This he affirmed in the words, " Lo, here is my signature, let the Almighty answer me." His position was that he had made his declaration, and signed it, notwithstanding the fact that he had not heard the charge which God had to make against him. There is a sense in which he was quite right. God had made no charge against him. He felt, however, that there must be such a charge to account for his experiences, and thus his last challenge was to God.

All this reveals the consciousness of a man that God was acting as Adversary, or Prosecutor, but that he did not know what the charge against him was. He had been listening to the chatter of his friends. Indeed, he had to listen to more, for Elihu will presently address him. In his consciousness he knew that these men were really not his judges, and had no right to bring any charge against him. He recognized that the only One Who had such a right was God Himself. This in itself was a great and true conviction. We have a striking illustration of it in the fifty-first Psalm, the great penitential Psalm of David, in which he said :

" Against Thee, Thee only, have I sinned."

So that the underlying consciousness of Job was that of the ultimate tribunal to which every man has a right to make his appeal.

The poignant agony of his soul at the moment was that it seemed to him that he was not getting a hearing in that court. In all the affairs of the human soul it is so that final judgment must be found by One Whose knowledge is perfect, and Whose decisions will be absolutely impartial and just. There is no court that fulfils this ideal perfectly, until the soul stands face to face with God. It was for this Job asked in this great appeal.

In a careful examination of the position, will be revealed the fact that this is the abiding challenge of the human soul. Of course, that is when God is recognized. If men dismiss God from the universe, all this has neither sense nor meaning. The cry of Job was the language of a man who believed in a moral universe over which God reigns, and in which He governs. Job, conscious of his innocence, appealed to God. David, conscious of his guilt, said,

"Against Thee, Thee only, have I sinned."

Whether the sense of innocence or the sense of guilt, the man, believing in a moral universe, makes his final appeal to this ultimate court, desiring to be judged there, and to accept the verdict found there. The truth is illustrated on another occasion in the history of David. When he had failed, and punishment was inevitable, he said,

"Let me not fall into the hand of man."

It was a most significant utterance. How constantly, under stress and strain of life, its perplexities and problems, and under the sense of sin, we desire to get beyond the thinking and the judgments of men, and to be dealt with directly by God.

Listening to the words of Job, the question that comes is as to whether we can have access to that court and stand before that Judge. In Job's words we hear the cry, the sigh, the sob, the revelation of necessity. Was there any answer to that cry?

Whereas we might reply to that inquiry by referring to the rest of the Book of Job, in which it is surely shown that God revealed Himself to Job as governing, and therefore available to himself ; we make our appeal rather to the answer that came after centuries had run their course historically.

There came into human history the Son of God, and through Him we find the complete answer to Job. That answer vindicates the cry he uttered, and says in effect ; Yes, it is possible to find the way to God, and to have immediate dealings with Him.

Out of a stupendous passage in the letter to the Hebrews we take these words, for the moment :

> " Ye are come . . . to God the Judge of all " ;

and then other words, revealing what we find in our coming :

> "And to Jesus, the Mediator of a new covenant " ;

Now in order to understand the value of these statements, we need to carefully observe the whole of the paragraph in which they are found:

> "Ye are come unto Mount Zion, and unto the city of the living God, the heavenly Jerusalem, and to innumerable hosts of angels, to the general assembly and Church of the Firstborn who are enrolled in heaven, and to God the Judge of all, and to the spirits of just men made perfect, and to Jesus the Mediator of a new covenant, and to the blood of sprinkling that speaketh better than that of Abel."

That passage in its entirety is an epitome of the new economy created by Jesus Christ. I use the word "economy" there, because it refers to the whole system of government. In the beginning of the letter to the Hebrews we read:

> "When He bringeth in the Firstborn into the world."

The word there rendered "world" is the word *oikoumene*, from which we derive our word "economy." It was the word that was used at the time in reference to the whole Roman Empire. This letter to the Hebrews is concerned from beginning to end with the new economy resulting from the speech of the Son ; and I repeat, that it is fully described in this paragraph which stands, as a description, in immediate contrast to that which has preceded it, namely, a description of the old economy under Moses. That economy was represented by

> " a mount that might be touched . . . that burned with fire, and . . . blackness, and darkness, and tempest, and the sound of a trumpet, and the voice of words ; which voice they that heard entreated that no word more might be spoken unto them ; for they could not endure that which was enjoined. If even a beast touch the mountain, it shall be stoned ; and so fearful was the appearance that Moses said, I exceedingly fear and quake."

That was the old economy, a Divine economy, an economy of God. The writer now says, however, " We are not come " to that. That is not where we stand to-day. " We are come unto Mount Zion," the economy of which he describes in the words already quoted.

The language descriptive of the new economy takes up the symbol of the old in certain ways. The new economy is that of Mount Zion. If we glance back to Hebrew poetry we find interpretations of Mount Zion. The second Psalm says that Mount Zion is the place of the King. The forty-seventh declares that Mount Zion is the joy of the whole earth. The seventy-eighth announces that Mount Zion is loved by Jehovah. The one hundred and twenty-fifth declares Mount Zion to be immovable, abiding for ever. Now the writer speaks of Mount Zion as being "the city of the living God, the heavenly Jerusalem."

In other words, he is declaring that through the Son we are brought into the realization of the Divine order and the Divine government. Every line of description is full of light and beauty.

The central fact, however, is the declaration that

> "We are come . . . unto God the Judge of all."

and that in that Presence, Jesus is the Mediator.

In the economy of the mount that burned with fire, God was the Judge of all. With a recognition of that abiding principle, the writer goes back to Abel, the shedding of whose blood was due to rebellion against God, and which therefore called for vengeance. In the new economy there is the shedding of blood, but it is not calling for vengeance, but rather for mercy and pardon. In the new economy we find our way to the judgment seat of God, but we do so through the mediation of His Son, in and through the shedding of His blood.

Thus the cry of the soul for access to God as ultimate Judge is answered, and the way is revealed as a way that provides for the deepest necessities of the soul, which have to do with its failure and its sin.

To that Throne for immediate judgment we may come now. Revelation has revealed to us the fact that there will be a great ultimate Assize, or day of judgment ; but we have not to wait for that day to find our way to the Throne. This is the full and final answer to the challenge of the human soul, as confessed by Job in his agony.

According to this story, God heard the cry, and came immediately, and talked to him. Even then He made no charge against him, except that of reminding him of his own limitations. Nevertheless, the complete revelation of the attitude of God towards the soul of man came with the coming of His Son into human life.

The ultimate value of this cry of Job is its expression of the deepest consciousness of a human being who recognizes that he lives in a moral universe. Necessarily if that be denied, there is no such cry, no such sense of appeal. Wherever there is this consciousness, there is also a sense of personal accountability. That sense may at the moment be a consciousness of innocence, or a conviction of guilt. In order to the ratification of the consciousness of innocence, the soul desires direct dealings with the God of the universe. That is equally true, and perhaps more poignantly so, if the consciousness be that of guilt. Human condemnation is of no moment in the last analysis, and human ability is utterly unable to deal with the situation.

Then it is to God that the soul inevitably

turns. It does so because it recognizes the
impotence and inadequacy of all human judgments and decisions. It passionately desires
to escape from all imperfect judgment. It
reaches out to the only One Who knows perfectly, and Who therefore will find the true
verdict, and pronounce the sentence which is
one of strict justice. Amid the often trivial
lilt of the words of Gilbert, I find some which
for some reason always appeal to me as very
full of significance. I refer to the lines,

> " I shall achieve in time,
>   My object all sublime,
> To make the punishment fit the crime,
>   The punishment fit the crime."

There is a gentle touch of sarcasm, and a tone
of merriment in the words, and yet they express
at least half the truth about what the soul of
man sincerely needs. We need that the punishment should fit the crime, and also that the
reward should be according to the innocence.
In other words and better, we need to be
judged by God.

It is a great thing for the human soul when
it ceases to listen to the opinion of neighbours,
and the arguments of philosophers, and the

futilities of the clever men of earth, and flings itself out into the clear light of the judgments and findings of God.

When any soul does that, it finds there, Jesus the Mediator of a new covenant, Whose blood makes possible the activity of mercy upon the basis of the strictest justice. Before that Throne, through the mediation of the Mediator, justice and mercy meet together, righteousness and peace kiss each other.

VIII

THE DISCOVERY OF SELF

" Behold, I am of small account."—Job xl. 4.

" What shall a man give in exchange for his life ? "—Matthew xvi. 26.

" God so loved the world that He gave His only begotten Son."—John iii. 16.

At this point in the Book of Job we find ourselves beyond the controversy between himself and his three friends. Their voices are silent. Moreover, the voice of the last speaker, Elihu, whose address proved that he had a profounder understanding of life than the other three, had been suddenly disturbed, and so silenced. His speech was cut short abruptly by the satire of heaven, as the voice of God was heard speaking out of the whirlwind,

" Who is this that darkeneth counsel
By words without knowledge ? "

Then immediately the Voice for which Job had been waiting, thus heard out of the whirlwind, silencing the last of his philosopher friends, addressed itself directly to Job, and began thus,

> " Gird up now thy loins like a man ;
> For I will demand of thee, and declare thou unto Me."

God addressed Job as an intelligent human personality, and in doing so ignored all the things of his circumstances. We can still picture Job sitting in his sorrow, stripped of everything upon which men naturally depend for the experiences and realizations of life ; his wealth gone, his children swept out, his health gone, the partnership of his wife in faith gone ; all his acquaintances absent ; and the little group of friends having utterly misunderstood him. So far as circumstances were concerned, he is seen as a derelict, possessing nothing.

The first words of God to him remind him that he still had his own personality :

> " Gird up now thy loins like a man."

Having thus called him to attention, the great Divine speech continued, and in it no reference was made to the sufferings of Job ; no explanation was offered of anything that had transpired. God offered him no philosophy to account for his position. What He did was to bring Job face to face with the universe in which he lived ; and then to ask him if he found himself able to govern that universe. That is a blunt summary of the speech of God, but it does give us the essential things thereof. Facing the universe, Job was brought to the consideration of inanimate life, and animate life ; to the contemplation of the movements of seasons, currents of wind, of snow and storm. Then he was asked whether he were equal, either to the creation of what he saw, or to its government. The point of the argument was an inquiry, seeing he could not do these things, how could he be equal to perfect understanding of God, or argument with Him.

In the light of that unveiling there came to Job a discovery of himself by comparison, and this great cry escaped him :

" Behold, I am of small account."

It is as though he had said, by comparison, I am nothing. What right have I to have made the protestations which have escaped my lips, or to claim that the God of the universe should

do anything for me ?   It was by comparison a
true vision of himself.

It is of the utmost importance that we understand correctly what Job really said.   The Old
Version rendered it :

" Behold, I am vile,"

which was a perfectly correct translation in
the time of King James, because then *vile*
did not mean what it has come to mean in the
process of the years.   In the Hebrew word
there is no suggestion of moral failure.   Quite
literally it means, of no weight.   Job did not
here in the presence of the majesty of God
confess moral perversity, but comparative insignificance.

David in one of his great songs expressed the
same sense of littleness :

" When I consider Thy heavens, the work
   of Thy fingers,
   The moon and the stars which Thou hast
      ordained ;
   What is man, that Thou art mindful of
      him ?
   And the son of man, that Thou visitest
      him ? "

In this song David revealed, in the very question he asked, his sense of the dignity of man, that he was one of whom God was mindful, and one whom He visited. Nevertheless it is the same sense of the greatness of God creating a consciousness of the comparative insignificance of personality.

The cry of Job was a great cry. God had called upon him to gird up his loins as a man, and he did so, and his greatness is seen in the fact that he was able to grasp in thought the greatness of God, and to make his comparison. When we say that we are unable to grasp the universe, the infinite, we really are showing that we have already done it. We cannot interpret all that lies within it ; but man's greatness lies in the fact that he can conceive the universe. The man who can say, " I am of small account," is proving in the saying that intellectually he grasps the idea of the universe, and of the Divine relation thereto. It is impossible to suggest the greatness of the universe to a dog. A dog has intelligence and emotion and will power. Indeed, it may be said that a dog has faith in his master ; but no dog can believe in anything beyond his immediate consciousness. No animal can grasp the idea of a universe. Man is able so to do, and in the doing of it is revealing the greatness and dignity of personality in itself. Was it not Kepler who said that all scientific investigation was proof of man's ability to think the thoughts of God after Him ? Nevertheless this unveiling of the majesty and power of God, while revealing the dignity of man in his ability to conceive of it, must inevitably produce in his mind the sense of his comparative insignificance. It was this that found expression in Job's declaration, " Behold, I am of small account."

We now turn to inquire what Jesus has to say to that consciousness in man ; and the first thing to be said is that never by any word He uttered did He agree that this declaration of Job is the final truth about man. He confronted men as He found them, with degraded conceptions of themselves, and He demanded that they deny, not the essential fact of their personality, but the sum-total of their thinking about themselves, resulting from their sin and rebellion against God. He did this, moreover, in order that they might discover the true majesty of their life according to Divine purpose. The mastery of Jesus which first humbles a man to the dust in abnegation, lifts him, when yielded to, into the realm of the glory and majesty of his being. That is but to summarize.

From the teaching of our Lord we take two statements, separated as to time of their utterance, but united in a revelation of a fundamental philosophy, as they give us two views which are complementary to each other. The first of these was His question :

> " What shall a man give in exchange for his life ? "

a question revealing His sense of the intrinsic value of a man. The other statement is that of the opening sentence of the great word of the Gospel :

> " God so loved the world that He gave His only begotten Son."

In that word we find a revelation of the value of a man in the thought of God.

As to the first :

> " What shall a man give in exchange for his life ? "

That question followed another :

> " What shall it profit a man if he gain the
> whole world, and forfeit his life ? "

In that question He employed the terms of
the market-place. He said in effect, Strike a
balance. On one side He placed the whole
world, and as we watch, we seem to see the
weight of the world, its values, its riches,
heavily weighting the scales. Now into the
other scale put a man ; and in the thought of
our Lord, the weight of the man is far more
than that of the world. The measure in which
men have at any time been able to possess the
world demonstrates the absolute truth of the
suggested comparison. Men have constantly
been busy attempting to " corner " things.
They have never been quite successful ; but
supposing, said Jesus in effect, that a man
could " corner " everything, and lose his soul
in the process, what would it profit him ?

" Behold, I am of small account," said Job.
The answer of Jesus is that taking a man, and
putting him into the balances, he is worth
more, and is weightier than the whole
world.

The second question of our Lord in this connection emphasizes the truth :

> " What shall a man give in exchange for his soul ? "

This question presumes that a man has sold himself, and so has lost his personality. The inquiry is as to what a man shall give to regain that which has been lost. There is no answer to the question. The Lord left it as an inquiry. If we face it, we discover its searching nature. If, peradventure, we have gained the world, and in the process lost our personality, what shall we give to regain that personality ? If we say we will give the world back for it, we discover that the thing lost is too valuable to be repurchased in that way. If we say we will give ourselves to regain ourselves, we are arguing in a vicious circle, for are we not sold, and so lost ?

It is interesting here to remind ourselves that before the controversy between Job and his friends, Satan uttered his opinion of a man, as he said :

> " All that a man hath will he give for his life."

Here Jesus was corroborating that by asking a question, What will he give ? " I am of small account," said this man in the long ago, as he gazed upon the majesty and the glory of God. Now the voice of God, speaking through His incarnate Son, says in effect, However true that may be, it is not all the truth.

Then when the question of Jesus has brought man face to face with the value of his own personality, and with the fact that if he have bartered it for anything, he has no means of buying it back, we hear Him declaring that

> " God so loved the world that He gave His only begotten Son."

That is God's vision of the worth of a man. The mystery of that is ineffable and unfathomable, but it remains a clear declaration and statement. To save men from utterly perishing, God gave His only begotten Son.

Standing in the midst of the universe, a being conscious of the majesty and the might of the wisdom and the power of God, I say with perfect honesty and accuracy, " I am of small account." Standing in the presence of the Son of God, and listening to His teaching, I find that I am of greater value than the whole world, and to the heart of God of such value, that in order to my recovery He gave His only begotten Son.

All that is so full of light as to be blinding; but Faber expressed the sense of it marvellously when he wrote:

> " How Thou canst think so well of us,
>   And be the God Thou art,
> Is darkness to my intellect,
>   But sunshine to my heart."

Right daringly, I would write four lines to accompany those of Faber, and I would write them thus:

> " And Thou dost think so well of us,
>   Because of what Thou art,
> Thy love illumes my intellect,
>   And fills with fear my heart ! "

We stand amid the beauty of the world and the glory of the sky and the majesty of the universe, and realize inevitably that, by comparison, we are of small account.

Yet, as David saw, God is mindful of us, and visits us; and when He visited us in the Son of His love, He came to reveal the fact to us that each individual of us is worth more than all the world, and are so dear to Him, that for our deliverance He gave His only begotten Son.

IX

THE DISCOVERY OF GOD

" I had heard of Thee by the hearing of the ear ;
But now mine eye seeth Thee,
Wherefore I abhor myself, and repent
In dust and ashes."—Job xlii. 5, 6.

" From that time began Jesus to preach, and to say,
Repent ye ; for the Kingdom of Heaven is at hand."—
Matthew iv. 17.

Our last meditation was concerned with the
cry of Job which revealed his discovery of himself. We now come to consider the cry which
resulted from his fuller discovery of God.

After he had come to consciousness of himself by comparison with the universe, and
consequently by comparison with the God of
the universe, that he was of small account, then
Jehovah continued, for He had more to say to
His servant.

This second movement in the speech of God
to Job began exactly as the first did :

" Gird up thy loins now like a man,
I will demand of thee, and declare thou
unto Me."

Job had said, " I am of small account." The reply of God was started by reminding him that he was a man, and calling upon him to behave like one. This method of approach on each occasion was a recognition of the dignity of man. Every man is driven to say, " I am of small account," when he stands in the presence of the God of the universe. That is a natural and inevitable consciousness ; and it might lead almost to a sense of despair. It is then as though God would remind him of the truth revealed in the account of the creation of man, in the words :

" Let us make man in Our image, after Our likeness."

Again it is as though God would say to him, There is none other in the earthly order to whom I can tell My secrets, or who can talk to Me. Thus even though we see Job in the midst of desolation, stripped of his belongings, his loved ones, and his wealth, misunderstood by his friends, we are looking at a being who, in God's estimate, is greater than all the creation, the glories of which had been made to pass before the afflicted man.

The argument and the appeal of this second address of God dealt with the one thing in which Job had indeed been foolish. That fact emerges in the words of God :

> " Wilt thou even disannul My judgment ?
> Wilt thou condemn Me, that thou mayest be justified ? "

In many ways it is true that Job had done no wrong, and said no wrong. He had not charged God foolishly, but he had questioned the justice of God, the government of God, the wisdom of God. These questionings had emerged time after time, in the magnificent and audacious honesty of the things he had said in his agony.

Here then he was sharply pulled up, as God asked whether he would disannul the judgment of God, whether Job intended to condemn God, that he might himself be justified.

In the stately beauty of the following address God is heard calling upon Job to assume the government. He did this with a satire as gentle as the kiss of a mother, when she laughs at a child. It is impossible to read it without feeling that it is full of that kind of tender laughter with which fathers and mothers often laugh at their children. There was no bitterness in it, no unkindness. With all the vision of the rhythmic order of the universe before Job, and while Job in his heart had been, and perhaps still was, questioning the government of God, he was asked if he was prepared to assume the government of the universe. Patently the suggested deduction was that if he were unequal to that, did he not at least find evidences in God's government which denied the fears that filled his heart?

It is arresting that this was the method of God with Job. He did not attempt to explain His method, but sought to create confidence therein, despite its mystery. He was thus bringing the man face to face with himself, and so face to face with his own personal disability.

God first asked Job if he were able to assume the government of affairs in the moral realm :

" Deck thyself now with excellency and
        dignity ;
    And array thyself with honour and
        majesty.
    Pour forth the overflowings of thine anger ;

And look upon every one that is proud,
   and abase him.
Look on every one that is proud, and
   bring him low ;
And tread down the wicked where they
   stand.
Hide them in the dust together ;
Bind their faces in the hidden place,
Then will I also confess of thee
That thine own right hand can save thee.''

The reading of that is sufficient, revealing the
fact that God was calling this man to face
the moral problem which had vexed him all
the way through, and to consider whether he
would be able to deal with such a problem.

No solution was offered, but in the method
of inquiry tremendous suggestions were made.
In effect God was saying to His servant, There
are things which must be allowed to work
themselves out ; while still all these matters
are under the Divine control, and are moving
towards the fulfilment of purpose, procession-
ally, by the necessities of the case, God is
Himself limited.

When I went in New York to see *Green*

Pastures I never shall forget the impression created upon my mind, as imaginatively but quite reverently, from the standpoint of negro mentality, the Lord is represented as viewing the world in revolt and in rebellion, and the angel Gabriel, in sympathy with God, desired to blow the trumpet, and call the judgment, and blot out the sinning earth, the Lord said to him, " Gabe, it ain't no picnic bein' Gawd! "

If for a moment that seems to shock the mind, let it be remembered that what I have said is true, that it was the negro outlook that expressed itself. If that be remembered, we are brought face to face with the very principle of the Cross.

When Job exclaimed, " Now mine eye seeth Thee," it ever seems to me that he had caught a vision, in the light of this moral problem, of God as a God of might, but of holiness also ; and there had come to him the realization of what in certain senses we may reverently describe as the difficulties of God.

Then once more for the sake of illustration, the speech of God moved out of the moral realm into that of the non-moral, that of the beasts and the animals. He called upon Job to look at two beasts, Behemoth, probably the hippopotamus ; and Leviathan, possibly the crocodile. I am aware that there are those who interpret these words as being pictorial or parabolic references to Satan and the underworld. That may be so. We will not argue it, but keep to the illustrations as employed. A study of the passage will show how remarkable is the accuracy of the description of these monsters. Now God asks Job if he is able to capture them, to domesticate them, to bring them under control. With regard to leviathan He says :

> " Lay thine hand upon him ;
> Remember the battle, and do so no more."

Surely it is impossible to read that without recognizing the humour of it.

Thus Job, having been compelled to face his own incompetence in the moral realm, is asked to face the fact of his equal incompetence in this realm of non-moral force.

After this speech of God to Job, he uttered the great cry that we are considering :

> " I had heard of Thee by the hearing of the
>   ear ;

But now mine eye seeth Thee,
Wherefor I abhor myself, and repent
In dust and ashes."

There had come to Job a new consciousness of God, revealing to him his own impotence. All the knowledge he had had of God, which had been revealed in his arguments with his philosopher friends, fell short of true apprehension. But now he had seen Him. The vision of God in the presence of moral delinquency had brought him to two definite conclusions, expressed in the words :

" Thou canst do all things,"

and

" No purpose of Thine can be restrained."

There came to him in the midst of his desolation, when all the props upon which he had leaned had gone, and when the voices of his friends had been silenced, a vision of God which brought conviction, not finally of difficulty, but of power ; a conviction, therefore, that in the long issue no purpose of God could be frustrated.

This new vision of God brought a new vision of himself. This was expressed in a statement which our translators have rendered, " I abhor myself." The revisers have substituted in the margin, " I loathe my words." Without any hesitation I say that neither rendering expresses the true thought. The word " myself " is not in the Hebrew, neither is the expression " my words." Moreover, the Hebrew word does noc signify a state of mind which can accurately be described either by the word " abhor " or " loathe." The Hebrew word literally means, from the standpoint of etymology, to disappear ; from the standpoint of usage, to retract, to repudiate. As a matter of fact, Job at this point went beyond what he had previously said when he declared, " I am of small account," and declared that he practically cancelled himself entirely. I disappear, I retract all that has been said ; I repudiate the position I have taken up. Then, restoring the sense of personality, he continued :

" I repent in dust and ashes."

The word here rendered " repent " is not the one that suggests a change of mind, but one that indicates sorrow.

Thus the language of Job was that of complete submission to God, and in that submission his own greatness was revealed and realized as nowhere else.

To go back for a moment, we call to mind Eliphaz's advice to him :

> " Acquaint now thyself with Him, and be
> at peace."

The reply of Job to that had revealed his difficulty at the moment :

> " Oh that I knew where I might find Him! "

Eliphaz, continuing to emphasize his advice, had urged him :

> " Lay thy treasure in the dust,
> And the gold of Ophir among the stones
> of the brooks."

Now Job said, not as the result of Eliphaz's appeal, but as the result of the unveiling of God before his astonished soul, I cancel myself, I am filled with sorrow. I lay all my treasure in the dust ; and in that moment Job rose to the ultimate dignity of his manhood. Tennyson's lines almost inevitably occur :

> " Our wills are ours, we know not how,
> Our wills are ours to make them Thine."

Man rises to the ultimate dignity, grandeur,

splendour of his own life when he recognizes that, and yields himself in complete submission to that will.

When we turn to ask what Jesus has to say to that cry of Job, we find the answer in the keynote of His ministry as declared in the words, that He " began . . . to preach, and to say, Repent ye ; for the Kingdom of heaven is at hand," as Matthew records. Mark recording the same fact uses slightly different language, saying that " Jesus came into Galilee preaching the Gospel of God, and saying, The time is fulfilled, and the Kingdom of God is at hand ; repent ye, and believe in the Gospel." In these two accounts we have two phrases, Matthew using " the Kingdom of heaven," and Mark, " the Kingdom of God." Matthew's phrase suggests an order of life, while Mark's indicates the authority producing the order. In that sense the phrases are synonymous. The fundamental fact, then, of the message of Jesus was that of a recognition of Divine authority, and of the order resulting from submission thereto. The way of entrance to the experience of the Kingdom of heaven is that of repentance ; and repentance in that sense

includes all that Job had said, the cancelling
of self in the presence of the consciousness of
the Divine authority :

When Paul wrote :

> " I have been crucified with Christ ; yet
> I live ; and yet no longer I, but Christ
> liveth in me ; and that life which I now
> live in the flesh I live in faith, the faith
> which is in the Son of God, Who loved
> me, and gave Himself up for me,"

he was revealing the fact that Christ had
brought him to the exact place that Job had
reached, with the difference that Job at the
moment only realized the negative, and waited
for the light of the positive.

God has many ways of breaking in upon the
consciousness of the human soul. We have
seen how He did so with Job. He comes in
other ways to other men. The result is always
the same, that the man thus brought face to
face with Him has to say, I disappear, and am
filled with sorrow. When man reaches that
place, God lifts him from the dust to the place
of fulness of life and experience.

The sense of peace which fills the soul as the

result of taking this place, and being brought
by God in understanding of himself, was simply
but finely expressed by Horatius Bonar :

> " Thy way, not mine, O Lord,
>   However dark it be ;
> Lead me by Thine own hand,
>   Choose out the path for me.
>
> Smooth let it be or rough,
>   It will be still the best ;
> Winding or straight, it leads
>   Right onward to Thy rest.
>
> I dare not choose my lot ;
>   I would not, if I might ;
> Choose Thou for me, my God ;
>   So shall I walk aright.
>
> Take Thou my cup, and it
>   With joy or sorrow fill.
> As best to Thee may seem ;
>   Choose Thou my good and ill ;
>
> Choose Thou for me my friends,
>   My sickness or my health ;
> Choose Thou my cares for me,
>   My poverty or wealth.
>
> Not mine, not mine the choice,
>   In things or great or small ;
> Be Thou my guide, my strength,
>   My wisdom, and my all."

That is indeed the language of the human soul
when it has come to full realization of the glory
and dignity of life in the vision of God.

X

THE SENSE OF SOLUTION

" He knoweth the way that I take,
When He hath tried me, I shall come forth as gold."

JOB xxiii. 10.

" Blessed is the man that endureth temptation ; for
when he hath been approved, he shall receive the crown of
life."—JAMES i. 12.

IN this last meditation in this series we pass
back to a word uttered in the second cycle of
the controversy of Job with his friends. In
previous studies we have followed a sequence.
In the course of that sequence I omitted this
cry, because in many ways it is most remarkable,
and the more so because of the deep darkness
in which Job was living at the time. It is
found at the point we have made reference to
more than once, when Eliphaz had uttered his
supreme word of advice :

" Acquaint now thyself with Him, and be
at peace " ;

And Job had replied :

" Oh that I knew where I might find Him! "

The supreme element in his anguish was that of his inability to make definite contact with God.

In considering that advice of Eliphaz, and the answer of Job, this tenth verse might be lifted out, without breaking in upon the continuity of Job's reply. The thing he said was most distinctly a parenthetical exclamation, welling up from the deeps of his being :

> " He knoweth the way that I take,
>   When He hath tried me, I shall come
>   forth as gold."

The cry revolves around two personalities, God and Job. In the whole of the book we meet with other personalities : Satan at the beginning ; then Eliphaz, Bildad, Zophar, and presently Elihu. In this cry none is in sight save the two referred to by pronouns :

> " *He* knoweth the way that *I* take,
>   When *He* hath tried *me*, *I* shall come
>   forth as gold."

Having uttered this cry, the gloom settled upon him immediately. We find him plunged back into the darkness almost of despair.

Nevertheless out of his deepest consciousness these words found utterance, and they reveal his sense of his own personality in relationship with God. In the previous controversy when answering Eliphaz, we find that Job had lost his sense of the dignity and worth of his own personality; and all he asked was that he should be blotted out. Now, in spite of this, this word was uttered.

In the cry the two things which are clearly manifest are those of his self-consciousness, and his consciousness of God. Two lights seem to have met, light on his personality, and light on the fact of God; and the two things are recognized as inter-related.

It is indeed a great revelation. A man is seen stripped, angry, and rebellious, standing up in the midst of his suffering, and his sense of inability to get into contact with God; and yet suddenly words fall from his lips which reveal truths of tremendous significance.

In the words, " He knoweth the way that I take," there is revealed the conviction that there was a way that he was taking. Here, however, we need to be careful in our consideration. The Hebrew word here rendered " way " does not suggest a journey, or a pathway. The marginal reading in the Revised throws light upon this :

" He knoweth the way that is with me."

That is to say, the reference is not to a pathway to be trodden, but to a potentiality resident within the being. The declaration means, then, that God knows all that is in a man; the ultimate meaning of individual personality.

We have some light upon that in the familiar words :

" Train up a child in the way he should go,
    And even when he is old he will not
        depart from it " ;

which should be rendered :

" Train up a child in his own way,
    And when he is old he will not depart
        from it."

That is to say, that in every child there is a potentiality; and training should be in order to the development of that.

That is what Job meant when he referred to the " way that is with me." He was conscious that there was a meaning in his being,

a potentiality and a purpose. This is at once
the greatest and the most baffling of convictions that ever comes to the human soul. It is
the fact to which the statement refers. What
the purpose is may be unknown, and the way
of fulfilment may not be understood. The
sense of it is almost overwhelming, for it ever
brings the consciousness of inability to perfectly
apprehend. The affirmation he made was that
God knew him perfectly, and all that was
within him.

To that he added the statement :

"When He hath tried me, I shall come
forth as gold."

The first value of that statement is that of his
recognition that the processes of life con-
stituted a testing for gold. Therein was a
recognition that within him was admixture of
alloy ; things that needed to be dealt with.

Concerning him, then, the words expressed
a consciousness that his life had a meaning
and a purpose ; and that in order to its realization there was the need of processes of testing
as by fire.

But the supreme wonder of the statement is

not that of its revelation of self-consciousness, but that of the sense of God which for the moment illuminated him.   Of God he said,

"*He* knoweth the way that I take."

In effect he declared his own ignorance of the purpose of his personality, and of the potentialities within him which would enable him to realize that purpose. But what he did not know was perfectly known to God.

It is here that humanity is so constantly breaking down. We think we know ourselves. We decide what we are going to be and to do. All this is not only permissible but valuable ; but, until we recognize that of ourselves our knowledge is partial and incomplete, we are in danger of making shipwreck of life. That which is by Divine creation in every human being does not find on the earth level its ultimate value. The way that is in me is linked to the life that lies beyond. All this is known to God. The potentialities within the human soul create, if rightly adjusted, perfect fitness for the ultimate fulfilment of purpose. When our Lord, in those final hours when death was approaching, looked back to the day of His birth, to the time when as a little Babe He came into the world, He said to Pilate :

> " To this end have I been born, and to this end am I come into the world, that I should bear witness unto the truth."

Thus He linked His birth with a purpose and a principle. The question that we should ask ourselves is as to whether we are doing that ; and the only answer possible is that we cannot do it. Here, then, is the final value of the statement that what we cannot do because we do not know, God is able to do because He perfectly knows.

Job's phrase, " When He hath tried me," carries us beyond the fact of the knowledge of God to the fact of His government, in order to the fulfilment of the potentialities which are perfectly known to Him. Malachi's words, " He sitteth as a refiner of silver," help us to an understanding of this idea. The refiner of silver sits by the furnace, tempering its fires, always in the interest of the refining process. For this passing moment, then, of supreme illumination, Job saw all the experiences through which he was passing as flames of fire, testing gold ; and he saw God sitting as the Refiner, presiding over the processes which finally should bring him forth as gold. The fires of the refiner do not destroy the essential, but only the alloy. The emergence of personality into its final dignity will result from the knowledge and the testing of the Divine government.

The full and final corroboration of these convictions came in and through Jesus. All the teaching of our Lord and of His holy apostles as found in the New Testament literature ratifies the convictions to which Job gave utterance. Our illustration of that teaching is taken from the Epistle of James. This letter was specially written for those who were passing through fires of suffering, and the statement we consider is that which, in crystallized form, supplies the answer of Jesus, ratifying the statement of Job :

> " Blessed is the man that endureth temptation ; for when he hath been approved he shall receive the crown of life."

A statement so startling finds its full interpretation in the whole letter. The vision presented to the view is that of God presiding over all the strange and often baffling experiences of suffering and of testing, even as by fire, and that with a definite purpose, that purpose being, as James puts it, that those who pass through the testing shall find the crown of life. This is the same idea as that expressed by Job in the words:

"I shall come forth as gold."

James describes it as the reception of the stephanos, or victor's crown; the coronation of life, the full realization of its meaning; the ultimate victory in experience.

This government of the process by God was in the mind of Paul when he said,

"There hath no temptation taken you but such as man can bear."

That is to say, that God "sitteth as a refiner of silver," and will allow no fire to harm that which is being tested. In this immediate connection Paul continued:

"God is faithful, Who will not suffer you to be tempted above that ye are able; but will with the temptation make also the way of escape, that ye may be able to endure."

Such testing is severe, and James declares, " Blessed is the man that endureth temptation." The meaning of the word " endureth " is literally to sit under. It describes the attitude of fortitude in the midst of the burning of the fires.

In concluding this series of meditations we find an arresting fact that the Book of Job is only twice referred to in the New Testament: once from the pen of Paul, and once from that of James.

Paul's reference occurs incidentally when he quotes the words of Eliphaz in his first address to Job :

> " He that taketh the wise in their craftiness."

It ever seems to me that there was a touch of satire in Paul's quoting Eliphaz, because Eliphaz was certainly taken in his own craftiness.

The other reference is in James (v. 11) :

> " Ye have heard of the patience of Job."

This reference from James is full of revelation. The word is not well rendered " patience." The revisers have substituted in the margin the word " endurance," which is correct. We do not know the patience of Job in our common acceptation of the word patience. He was anything but patient. It is true that in the passage where the reference is found, James was urging patience, and he spoke of the patience of prophets, and of the endurance of Job. The two things are, of course, intimately connected. Patience, which means long-suffering, has reference to persons ; whereas endurance, which means staying under, has reference rather to an attitude towards circumstances.

I repeat, Job did not manifest patience in the sense of long-suffering. He was angry with his friends. He employed magnificent maledictory language when dealing with them. But Job did endure.

In the whole story of Job we see the patience of God, and the endurance of man. When these act in fellowship, the issue is certain. It is that of the coming forth from the fire as gold, that of the receiving of the crown of life. Adelaide Procter expressed the truth in her lines :

> " Let thy gold be cast in the furnace,
>   Thy red gold, precious and bright,
>   Do not fear the hungry fire,
>   With its caverns of burning light ;

And thy gold shall return more precious,
  Free from every spot and stain ;
For gold must be tried by fire,
  As a heart must be tried by pain !

In the cruel fire of Sorrow
  Cast thy heart, do not faint or wail ;
Let thy hand be firm and steady,
  Do not let thy spirit quail ;
But wait till the trial is over,
  And take thy heart again ;
For as gold is tried by fire,
  So a heart must be tried by pain !

I shall know by the gleam and glitter
  Of the golden chain you wear,
By your heart's calm strength in loving,
  Of the fire they have had to bear.
Beat on, true heart, for ever ;
  Shine bright, strong golden chain ;
And bless the cleansing fire,
  And the furnace of living pain ! "